GREAT MEAT
COOKERY

GREAT MEAT
COOKERY

EDITED BY TONY DE ANGELI

HAMLYN

NOTES

1. All spoon measurements are level. Standard spoon
measurements are used in all recipes:
1 tablespoon = one 15 ml spoon
1 teaspoon = one 5 ml spoon

2. All eggs are size two unless otherwise stated.

3. Metric and imperial measurements have been calculated
separately. Use one set of measurements only as they are not
exact equivalents.

4. Ovens should be preheated to the specified temperature.

Title spread illustration: Pork fillets and shredded pink
leeks with a port sauce (page 113)

First published in 1989 by The Hamlyn Publishing Group Limited,
a division of the Octopus Publishing Group,
Michelin House, 81 Fulham Road, London SW3 6RB.

© 1989 The Hamlyn Publishing Group Limited and The Meat and
Livestock Commission

ISBN 0 600 56510 6

Printed in Spain

CONTENTS

INTRODUCTION
BY
TONY DE ANGELI

When I was asked to devise and edit a book about one of our greatest institutions, the flattery soon gave way to apprehension. It felt a little like being asked to rediscover roast beef!

However, there is always an opportunity to be different, and we soon realised that altering some of the usual ingredients might produce a brand new recipe.

Curiosity is a great motivator. In fact, it makes professional cooks and the many millions of us amateurs want to create new dishes and variations. The most flattering question to a hostess is: 'Can you give me the recipe?' – the perfect example of two curious people coming to terms.

And what other people eat is fascinating. Would you not expect the Prime Minister's favourite recipe to include roast beef? Or the Leader of the Opposition's, Welsh lamb? Now you can find out. You will probably have guessed correctly in one case. But which one?

We decided to ask some 60 notables – men and women who have influenced our lives either through politics, cooking, writing, TV or radio – for their favourite meat dishes. Some of these personalities are nationally known, others have created a niche regionally. It might also be fun to imagine the authors' character by studying their choices. For example, for those who hate wastage, I strongly recommend Janet Cooper's leftover mutton pie (need I say more?). And Geoffrey John, very much an interested party as head of the Meat & Livestock Commission, came up with something from his Welsh roots. Cooking it is not difficult – but try pronouncing it!

What turns on a renowned cook used to producing hundreds of meat dishes? The answer could be pork chops, like you have never had before, or Manti – which you have never heard about before.

The recipes make a good browse because most of them are geared for everyday meals and specific occasions – like parties, family suppers, even camp-fire get-togethers.

So this book has many purposes. One of its prime functions is to trigger more interest in cooking at home, to help families enjoy what is a common pleasurable experience.

It is not a promotional device to double the sales of meat, to make us eat it twice a day, or to prove it is better than any other food.

The logic is very simple. More people eat meat than any other food. Meat also has a primary place in a balanced diet, and it is most enjoyable. And among the three main red varieties – beef, pork and lamb – there is an infinite number of cuts and recipes to keep hundreds of cookery writers going for ever, particularly as the industry has responded to changing public demands.

Total consumption of meat in the UK was around 3.9 million tonnes in 1987 – some 2% more than in 1986 – and the highest figure for over 20 years. But that included what we eat at home, in restaurants and fast food shops, and products made by manufacturers – canned and frozen.

It is no secret that the family lunch or dinner – seven or eight round a table tucking into the roast and three veg, followed by pudding and custard – is not as frequent as it used to be. Now, mothers have to prepare three or four

quick meals, as various members of the family rush in and out, all requiring different sorts of food. The age of convenience has not done much to advance the use of the oven or dining room.

However, amongst the alternatives are a whole range of new meat cuts which began when the Meat and Livestock Commission realised the industry had to change. The result is leaner steaks and joints and all sorts of almost-prepared products such as ground and minced meat in seasoned parcels, kebabs, beef olives – flattened pieces of meat ready for stuffing and rolling . . .

Susan (my wife) has just walked into the midst of this writing. 'Have you noticed any great changes in what you buy at the butcher's?' I asked innocently, hoping her reply would help this chapter along.

'Yes,' she said positively. 'I can buy all sorts of things I couldn't before, or I used to have to order specially . . .' 'For instance?'

'We had a crown of roast lamb last Saturday, remember?' 'Yes.' I admitted. 'Well, I bought it in the supermarket,' she said. 'And remember all that trouble I used to have making moussaka – I had to mince the lamb. Now I buy minced lamb. And what about veal escalopes, pork loin slices, spare ribs and lamb steaks cut off the end of the leg?'

I thanked her for the extra 100 words and then thought of the various boneless cuts of pork, ready rolled roasts, trimmed meats and the displays which are so much like the more imaginative Continental presentations, all part of a response that is keeping meat in its rightful place.

Cooking and eating the very best British meat is a joy – but it can become too much of a mystical experience. Some are frightened of the complication, especially when they read the dozen or so ingredients. All the recipes in this book have been tested but we can't guarantee the accuracy of the equipment in your kitchen or the way you cook. So, don't worry if you leave one or two ingredients out, or you substitute something. Also, don't fret too much about precise cooking times and temperatures – use your judgement as well. I have a theory that most ovens begin to lie at around 180°C, 350°F or Gas Mark 4 and never tell the truth about how quickly they are going to cook a 1.75 kg/4 lb joint.

Incidentally, a few days after writing the paragraph above, I heard a leading chef on radio say the same sort of thing. He advocated using an oven thermometer. And he also gave the often forgotten advice that roast meat should be 'rested' for 20 minutes or so before carving. Wrap it in foil to keep it hot. This really does increase tenderness. And, another tip: don't salt raw meat as it makes the blood run. Add to taste – on the plate.

But back to these recipes . . .

You can improvise provided you follow the basic rules and directions. I have a good example which resulted in a brand new dish being launched into the sophisticated dinner party world.

Susan cooks a delicious garlic shoulder of lamb. Basically, all you need is the meat, two crushed garlic cloves, salt and pepper, one tablespoon of mustard, another of dry ginger and two of flour. Mix up the dry ingredients, sprinkle it on the meat and cook. Baste about three times.

But before doing this you have to make a lovely gravy that goes with it. Put in a jug four tablespoons of Worcester sauce, plus the same amount of mushroom ketchup, and any brown sauce (yes, don't scream – out of a bottle), two tablespoons of sugar, one of vinegar, 25 g/1 oz of melted butter, cayenne, salt, 150 ml/$\frac{1}{4}$ pint of water, and a small onion finely sliced, which you put in last into the mixture. Give it a good whirl and then pour on to the meat.

We set our oven at 220°C, 425°F Gas Mark 7 for about 30 minutes and then switch down to 180°C, 350°F, Gas Mark 4. It takes about 30 minutes to 450 g/1 lb.

Now, that is simple enough, but cutting shoulder of lamb is not easy, even with a sharp knife in the right hand and directions in the left. The last time I was doing this, I became exasperated and inevitably I began to tear the meat from the bone. And then a great thought came. I was reminded of the Peking duck I had eaten in a Chinese restaurant the week before when the bird was beautifully shredded at the table by the waitress . . . Why not give the lamb the same treatment? And that is what I did.

The meat came off the bone as easily as peeling a banana, and placed in serried ranks on the large serving plate, even looked like Peking duck. With the sauce – fat skimmed off then poured out of the basting tin into a boat – the combination won at least three brownie points.

I only mention it to prove how cooking meat does not have to follow slavish rules. And anyway, why should I not be allowed a recipe alongside the Prime Minister, Jimmy Young and Claire Rayner?

The wonderful advantage of meat is that there is enough variety to suit different pockets, tastes and diets. Every Thursday I see the computer sheets that analyse prices in some 366 shops in 42 UK towns. The range in the same cuts is startling as shown in a recent week: beef boneless sirloin went from a low of 208p per 450 g/1 lb to 404p; lamb loin chops ranged from 169p to 248p per 450 g/1 lb and whole leg of pork was a bargain at 89p per 450 g/1 lb compared with 128p elsewhere.

There is not one single item that has a standard price. The reason is simple. Meat is not a branded product like baked beans or jam. Butchers and supermarket operators select particular cuts as specials, deciding particular prices to suit their customers, their marketing strategy, and their overall profit mix. And they change them frequently. They gain on the swings and lose on the roundabouts; their competitors do the same – but they use different swings and roundabouts.

The advice has to be: shop with your eyes and memory before making a choice. And be prepared to change your mind at the last minute; particularly as the abundance of choice is still growing.

There is no accounting for taste. Why do some like beef rare and others well-cooked? I have a brother-in-law who trims off the minutest particles of fat, and yet many believe without it there is no succulence. Perhaps there are so many preferences because there are so many choices.

In the rush-about-world where speed is of the essence, the minute steak stands supreme (in my view) as the Gold Medal snack. If you use a small, non-stick pan or grill, and slap the result between two slices of bread (don't forget salt, black pepper or mustard) you have a convenience meal that can be eaten while you answer the 'phone or paint the ceiling.

On the other hand, you may want to prepare one of the many classic recipes that deserve love, time, attention, good company, and a wonderful feeling of satisfaction.

This part of the book has been put into the capable hands of Rosemary Wadey, who is not only a very experienced cook and home economist but an accomplished writer. She was head of the Food Advisory Department of the Good Housekeeping Institute for some time and has written a number of books, including the Hamlyn Cookery Course (co-author), Cooking for Two and Cooking for Christmas.

Her section includes recipes from around Britain which deserve a greater national acceptance: The home economists on the British Meat team have provided classic dishes and added a few imaginative touches. You may be surprised to see quite a few foreign recipes. Admittedly, we did intend to be chauvinistic about British Meat – but not about what you do with it.

However, there is a section that more than makes up for any classic foreign influence. We ran a series of competitions in regional newspapers throughout the country to discover the best local, truly British, meaty meals, and we also approached heads of various organisations for their favourites. The result is a splendidly wide ranging number of dishes which deserve to travel well.

The names have a certain magic about them: Boozy Cockled Beef, for example, has a triple appeal that isn't clear until you read the instructions. And the suggestions include quickies like an interesting way of making a kidney sandwich spiced with creamed horseradish sauce.

There are also chapters about the background to a product that we perhaps take too much for granted. British meat comes from an industry that is known for its efficiency throughout the world, and what is more, it has set quality standards that are envied. But before we start cooking, we have to know the basic facts about meat – not just which part of the beast it comes from but how to trim, prepare, store and freeze it.

Unfortunately, there is a great deal that is not taught at school – or anywhere else. Where does a rump steak begin and end? Where is the fillet? Are the legs of lamb you eat, from the front or rear of the animal? Or both? Agreed, you don't have to be a doctor to enjoy a pork chop, but it helps if you begin with the knowledge that our grannies had.

Meat is extremely well-produced and deserves care and attention in the buying and preparation. So we have done our best to cover these areas in special introductory chapters.

It is also important to accept that eating should be a pleasure. Good company, good wine and good food go well together, and I am not just talking about parties.

Meat has been part of this happy scenario for centuries and undoubtedly this will continue. Just how much of it you eat and how often, is not my concern. Making the most of a nutritious, succulent, tasteful product, that can be treated in a myriad of ways, is what this book is about.

The problem with books of this kind is that the people who buy them don't need conversion, but they do make wonderful disciples.

By passing on their enthusiasm and their skills, they will ensure that Britain's great meat traditions will live on. By they, I of course mean you.

Tony de Angeli

CHOOSING
and
COOKING
BEEF
and VEAL

O f all British meats, beef is top favourite, undoubtedly because of its great versatility. There are cuts of beef for roasting, pot-roasting, casseroling, grilling, frying, boiling, barbecuing or microwaving – enough to produce a different meal every day of the week. Beef comes in large pieces such as the splendid joint which has long been the traditional centrepiece of the British Sunday lunch and in smaller, quick-to-cook cuts such as the steaks which are as important in the well-balanced diets of people as diverse in their food requirements as slimmers and very physically active people as they are in the diets of many ordinary, busy men and women.

This high-quality beef comes to us from retailers – both butchers and the supermarkets where more and more of us regularly buy our beef – in convenient forms intended to make life easier for the busy housewife and cook. Thus, alongside the traditional joints and cuts, there are beef ready-cubed for casseroles, goulashes and kebabs, thin slices of topside perfect for beef olives and lean beef minced ready for beefburgers, cottage pies, pasta sauces, chilli con carne, and many other dishes.

Britain's meat producers have answered the needs of our busy, health-conscious lifestyle by developing new leaner, tender cuts of beef, both from such quintessentially British breeds as the Hereford, Aberdeen Angus and Welsh Black and from a judicious introduction of Contintental breeds like the Charolais, Limousin and Simmental.

This beef is superbly nutritious. It is a good source of high biological value, easily digestible protein, making it an excellent food for growth, repair and building of body tissues. It contains more iron than other meats and in a form easily absorbed by the body; it is a good source of the B vitamins thiamin, nicotinc acid and riboflavin; and it contains vitamin B12, a vitamin which helps prevent anaemia and which is not found in foods of vegetable origin.

Today's beef has a low fat content and is low in calories. The actual number of calories in a given piece of beef will vary according to the amount of visible fat, cut and cooking method. On average, 100 g of lean roasted topside of beef contains 156 calories; estimate 173 calories for lean boiled silverside; and 218 calories for grilled rump steak with an edging of fat.

British beef, which is of the very highest quality, accounts for most of the beef eaten in this country, and we are now almost self-sufficient in it.

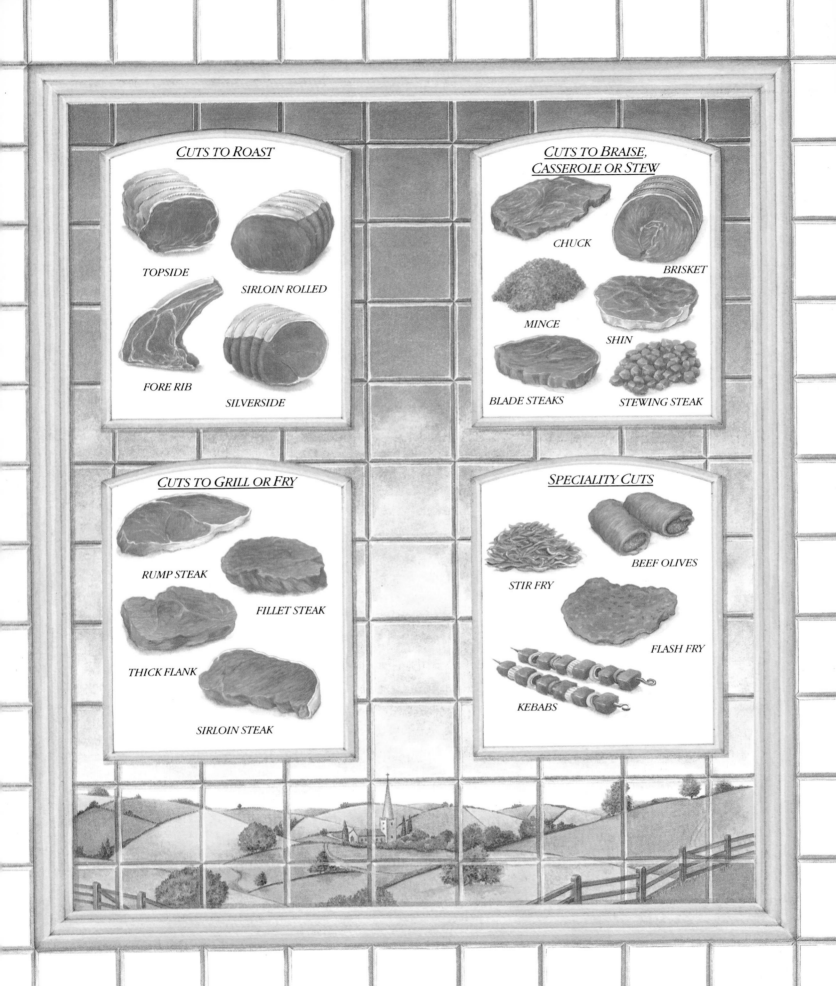

HOW TO COOK BEEF

Beef must be cooked in a way appropriate to its type: less tender cuts of beef need slow, moist cooking, such as casseroling, while beef with less connective tissue may be cooked quickly at high temperatures.

Roasting

Roasting is really a form of baking, in which the meat is cooked uncovered and dry (though it may be basted, usually with the pan juices and drippings, during cooking). Moderate temperature roasting is best suited to most joints, providing succulent, tender beef with less shrinkage. The more traditional high temperature roasting is best suited to top-quality joints. The thickness of the joint affects the rate of heat penetration, so that a thinner joint will cook more quickly than a thicker one.

To estimate roasting times as accurately as possible, the joint should be weighed after it has been prepared for cooking.

A really accurate way of judging when a joint is cooked to your liking is to use a meat thermometer with the probes inserted right to the centre of the joint about 10 minutes before the end of the calculated cooking time. Meat thermometer readings for beef (either with bone or boneless) are: well done – 80°C/175°F; medium – 70°C/160°F; rare – 60°C/140°F.

When *spit-roasting*, allow 15 minutes per 450 g/1 lb, plus 15 minutes extra.

TOPSIDE A very lean cut of beef with little or no fat, so it is often sold with a layer of fat tied around it to prevent it drying out during cooking. Traditionally it is a roasting joint, but is also very good pot-roasted as a joint, braised in slices, and cut into thin slices, beaten and formed into beef olives when it is braised or casseroled.

SIRLOIN The favourite roasting joint for many people when boned and rolled. It is particularly tender and succulent. It is sometimes sold with the undercut, or fillet, still attached. Otherwise, the fillet is removed from inside the backbone to be sold separately as fillet steak, either whole or in slices. Also very good when roasted on the bone. Rolled sirloin can be cut to any size; on the bone it has to be cut between the bones. Sirloin steaks are cut from this joint to grill or fry.

FORE RIB The traditional cut of Roast Beef of Old England. Sold on the bone, cut to the size you require, between the rib bones, or off the bone and rolled, according to taste. Served hot or cold, it makes an excellent centre piece. Excellent flavour.

WING RIB A popular roasting joint from the end of the ribs, so it is often cut to a triangular shape in varying sizes depending on the number of bones required. Also sold boned and rolled. Good steaks can be cut from this joint to grill or fry. Usually less deep in size than the other rib joints.

SILVERSIDE OR ROUND This is a good roasting joint but it needs plenty of basting as it is a very lean joint prone to drying out. Always sold boned, it is the traditional joint to be salted to cook as 'Boiled Beef and Carrots'. Also suitable to braise and pot roast.

AITCHBONE A lean joint sometimes called top rump which is next to the silverside and topside. The joint is very good for roasting with plenty of flavour. Can be braised and pot-roasted and salted ready to boil.

Pot Roasting

With this method, the joint is cooked gently with fat in a closed container, which may be a covered casserole, a covering of foil round the joint or a roasting bag, all of which will provide a moister atmosphere than roasting. The roasting times in the chart on page 12 do not apply to pot roasting.

BRISKET This joint has an excellent flavour but needs slow cooking. Sold either on the bone, or more usually boned and rolled.

ROASTING TIMES FOR BEEF		
TYPE OF JOINT	SLOW METHOD Moderately hot oven (190°C/375°F, Gas Mark 5)	FAST METHOD Hot oven (220°C/425°F, Gas Mark 7)
Meat on the bone		
Rare	20 mins per 450 g/1 lb plus 20 mins	15 mins per 450 g/1 lb plus 15 mins
Medium	25 mins per 450 g/1 lb plus 25 mins	20 mins per 450 g/1 lb plus 20 mins
Well done	30 mins per 450 g/1 lb plus 30 mins	25–30 mins per 450 g/1 lb plus 25 mins
Meat, boned and rolled		
Rare	25 mins per 450 g/1 lb plus 25 mins	20 mins per 450 g/1 lb plus 20 mins
Medium	30 mins per 450 g/1 lb plus 30 mins	25 mins per 450 g/1 lb plus 25 mins
Well done	35–40 mins per 450 g/1 lb plus 35 mins	30–35 mins per 450 g/1 lb plus 30 mins

It is also often salted or pickled to be gently boiled. Best if fried to brown all over and then pot roasted with vegetables and a certain amount of liquid; otherwise boil it slowly with flavouring vegetables. Suitable to serve hot or cold.

THICK FLANK A lean joint below the topside, which provides an excellent flavoursome and tender joint when pot-roasted or sliced and braised. It can also be thinly sliced to fry.

AITCHBONE As already stated excellent when pot-roasted or roasted.

TOPSIDE For those who think roast topside is a little dry or hard, try pot roasting for very succulent results.

Boiling
Beef cooked by this method is not 'boiled' but gently simmered, since true boiling would make the meat tough. It is cooked, completely covered with fresh cold water, in a saucepan with a well fitting lid to minimise water evaporation. Vegetables, herbs and spices are added to give the beef extra flavour and to make a tasty stock of the cooking liquid.

Cooking time is 25 minutes per 450 g/1 lb plus 30 minutes for large joints and about 1½ hours for small ones. If the beef is to be served cold it should be cooled in the cooking liquid. Using a pressure cooker cuts down the cooking time by about two-thirds and less water is needed.

Joints most often boiled are salted beefs – silverside and brisket. These may need several hours' or overnight soaking before cooking in fresh water.

Braising, Stewing and Casseroling
Beef that is braised is cooked by a combination of stewing, steaming and roasting, with the browned and sealed meat usually set on a layer of vegetables in a covered pan and cooked with just sufficient liquid to provide steam to keep the meat moist.

Casseroling, or stewing, is a slow, moist method of cooking, ideal for less tender, more economical cuts of beef. Herbs and vegetables are usually added for extra flavour and goodness. The ideal oven temperature is 160°C, 325°F Gas Mark 3. Casseroles simmered on top of the stove could have a heat-distributing mat under them. Meat labelled 'stewing' will need longer, slower cooking than meat labelled 'braising'.

CHUCK AND BLADE STEAK A large fairly lean cut of good quality meat which is removed from the bone to be sold as 'chuck steak' said to be the best for braising, casseroles, stewing, pie fillings etc, when either cut into cubes or individual portion sizes. This flesh may well be marbled with streaks of fat through it, but should not have too much external fat attached to it. Blade bone steaks can be treated to use as flash fry steaks or for braising.

THIN FLANK Found between the rump and the brisket, this is very good for braising and stewing; can also be bought salted or pickled and as best mince.

BRISKET Used for braising, stewing and pot roasting.

SHIN (foreleg) **AND LEG** (hindleg) Both are lean meat with a high proportion of connective tissue. The cheapest of all cuts, they are suitable for stews, casseroles, stock and soup. Without long cooking, it will be very tough, but the flavour is always good.

NECK AND CLOD Usually cut into pieces and sold for cooking as 'stewing steak' Most often used to make mince. It is lean but has less flavour and is less gelatinous than shin.

THIN AND THICK RIBS Usually sold boned and rolled to braise, or cut into slices (thin rib) for braising or into cubes for casseroles and stews.

SLICED TOPSIDE Thin slices, beaten thinly between sheets of greaseproof paper or cling film are rolled up with a stuffing for Beef Olives to braise or casserole.

Grilling and Frying
Grilling is a quick and easy way of cooking beef using dry heat, while frying, also quick and easy, involves a certain amount of fat. Grilling is, therefore, generally a healthier way of cooking beef quickly, though frying may enhance the succulence of very lean cuts. It is ideal for thin, tender cuts of beef, chops, kebabs and beefburgers. Barbecuing, a form of grilling, is also suitable for these cuts.

Marinades made of wine, vinegar or fruit juices, are often used with beef for grilling or barbecuing. They improve the tenderness of diced or thinly sliced meat. Flavoured marinades can also give the meat an extra flavour too.

Cooking times for grilling, frying and barbecuing will depend on the thickness of the beef being cooked and on how rare or well done it is wanted. A steak wanted 'rare' may require as little as 2½ minutes each side, for instance, while the same steak might need 6 minutes to be 'well done' right through.

Temperatures may vary, too: use a preheated, very hot grill for very tender meats such as fillet, sirloin or rump steak, but use a lower temperature for chops, cutlets and sausages.

RUMP STEAK An excellent lean and tender cut with a thin edging of fat, usually sold in slices of varying thicknesses for grilling and frying.

FILLET STEAK The undercut or fillet is found beneath the backbone under the sirloin. It has no fat at all and can be cooked whole; as the thick end for a joint called a Chateaubriand to roast or grill; or in steaks of varying thicknesses to grill or fry. It is an expensive but delicious steak.

SIRLOIN These steaks are cut from the boned sirloin joint and are one of the best flavoured.

FLANK STEAK The cheapest of the steaks which need to be well beaten first to ensure they are tender.

OTHER STEAKS Large steaks known as T-bone, and Porterhouse are good flavoured and tender but need a large appetite; entrecote are thin steaks and mignon are even thinner both of which need only short cooking and are often used in dishes such as Steak Diane. 'Flash fry' steaks are lean cuts of beef which have been passed between knife covered rollers to tenderize the meat and reduce the cooking time so they can be quickly (flash) fried; good flavour and economical. So-called 'minute' steaks are thin slices of tender, quick-cooking beef.

KEBABS These are cut from pieces of thick flank, topside, aitchbone etc ready for kebabs. Best if marinated first and then ready to grill. Sometimes bought ready threaded on to skewers ready to cook.

STIR FRY MIXTURES Again lean pieces of beef such as those used for kebabs, cut into narrow strips and mixed with special blends of herbs, spices and vegetables by the butcher, ready to take home and quickly create your own stir-fry meal.

VEAL

Veal is produced in relatively small quantities in Britain and is particularly favoured by the catering trade because of its delicate flavour, tender texture and the fact that it requires less cooking than beef.

There are two types of veal: milk-fed and grass-fed. Milk-fed veal is the more expensive but grass-fed is more plentiful and often thought to have the better flavour.

Veal should be soft, moist and very pale pink with barely any fat around it. Instead, there is a gelatinous tissue which softens when it is cooked. There is a little fat around the kidneys which is pure white.

The bones are pinkish-white and rather soft and are excellent for stock-making for they produce a large amount of jelly when boiled. The nutrients of veal are similar to beef. As it has very little fat, the flesh tends to dry out rather easily during cooking and it is better to use a moist method of cooking rather than plain roasting or grilling.

COOKING BEEF IN THE MICROWAVE

Cooking beef in a microwave oven is time-saving and economical and is successful, provided the basic rules for microwaving foods are observed. In the microwave cooking chart below the times were tested in a 650–700 watt cooker. Use these tables as a guide, but always check with your own cooker's handbook. For cookers with a lower wattage, add a few minutes to the cooking times given.

CUT	TIME FOR 450 g/1 lb	STANDING TIME	SPECIAL POINTS
Topside	5 mins rare 6–7 mins medium 8–10 mins well done	15–20 mins	Cook on full power.
Sirloin	5 mins rare 6–7 mins medium 8–10 mins well done	15–30 mins	Cook on full power.
Rib of beef, boned/rolled	6 mins rare 7–8 mins medium 8–10 mins well done	15–30 mins	Cook on 70%.
Minced Beef with vegetables	3 mins full power +18 mins – 50% power		Stir occasionally to avoid mince sticking together in lumps.
Rump steak	2 mins rare 2–4 mins medium/rare 4 mins well done		Use the browning dish. Times are for full power.
Fillet steak	2 mins rare 2–3 mins medium rare 3–4 mins well done		Use the browning dish. Times are for full power.

AVERAGE AMOUNTS OF BEEF TO ALLOW

TYPES OF MEAT	AMOUNTS PER PERSON
Beef on the bone	225–350 g/8–12 oz per person, plus a little extra for some to serve cold.
Boned and rolled beef	about 175 g/6 oz per person, plus a little extra to serve cold.
Steaks	150–224 g/5–8 oz per person, to suit your taste.
Casserole meat	about 175 g/6 oz per person.
Minced beef	100–150 g/4–5 oz per person.

TRADITIONAL ROAST BEEF

prime joint of beef on the bone e.g.
  sirloin, ribs (1.5–1.75 kg/3–4 lb) or a
  boned and rolled joint of sirloin, ribs,
  topside
25–50 g/1–2 oz dripping or oil
salt and black pepper
1 garlic clove (optional)

Accompaniments
Yorkshire puddings (see right)
Roast potatoes
Horseradish sauce
green vegetables
gravy

Preheat the oven to hot (220°C, 425°F, Gas Mark 7).

Wipe the joint and trim if necessary. Weigh and calculate the cooking time from the chart on page 12. Place in a roasting tin with the fat upwards. Season lightly, if liked, and rub with a cut or crushed clove of garlic.

Cook in the preheated hot oven for the calculated time.

Baste several times during cooking and roast potatoes around the joint for the last hour or so of cooking time.

Serve with roast potatoes, Yorkshire Puddings, Horseradish cream or sauce, gravy made from the pan juices and green vegetables.

SERVES 4–6

YORKSHIRE PUDDINGS

50 g/2 oz plain flour
pinch of salt
1 egg
150 ml/¼ pint milk

Sift the flour and salt into a bowl and make a well in the centre. Add the egg and gradually beat in the milk to give a smooth batter.

Add a little dripping or oil to 10–12 patty tins and put into the oven below the meat until the fat is really hot.

Pour the batter into the tins so they are not more than ¾ full and cook below the meat for about 20 minutes or until well puffed up and browned.
Serve hot.

CARVING AND SERVING BEEF

Take the meat out of the oven or off the heat to let it 'rest' for at least 5 minutes and up to 15 minutes before carving. This allows it to settle and makes carving much easier.

Always stand up to carve a joint – it is so much easier than trying to do it sitting down. Make sure the carving knife is really well sharpened before carving so that the blade will slide through the meat rather than sawing and tearing at the fibres. You may need to keep the knife sharpener to hand so that you can resharpen the blade regularly. Use a two-pronged carving fork with a finger guard to hold the joint still as you carve it.

Remove any string and/or skewers which will be in the way as you carve.

Stand the joint on a flat, non-slip surface such as a wooden board or a plate with spikes to hold it in position.

Remove any outer bones, which will be in the way of carving, but not the main bone to which the flesh is attached.

Cut across the 'grain' of the lean, in order to shorten the fibres. Usually, this means cutting at right angles to the bone.

WING RIB Remove the chine bone at the thickest end of the joint and lay the meat, fat uppermost, on a flat surface; then carve in narrow slices, loosening it from the rib bones as you go.

Carving a fore rib on the bone

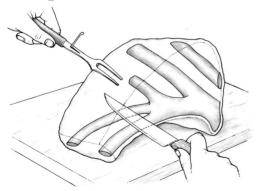

1 Run a sharp knife between the meat and the ribs

RIB ROASTS Remove any string and stand the joint on its wide end, holding it securely with a carving fork. If necessary, remove the chine bone with a sharp knife. Cut across the joint in even, fairly thick slices until the blade of the knife reaches the rib bone. Cut down close to the bone to loosen each slice.

BONED AND ROLLED JOINTS These should be carved across the grain and, if possible, carve on a board after removing skewers and string as necessary.

Beef may be served with many different sauces, vegetables, garnishes and other accompaniments, and different combinations will give quite surprising variations in taste, style and 'atmosphere'.

Choice of cooking method and the nature of the accompaniments can make considerable differences in the nutritional balance of a beef meal. Serve a grilled steak with grilled tomatoes and green salad, perhaps, and you will have quite a light meal, low in calories. Fry the same steak and serve it with fried mushrooms, chips and buttered peas for a heavier meal.

Most fresh vegetables do more than just complement beef; they add fibre and extra vitamins to the meal.

Over the years, various sauces and garnishes have become traditional for serving with beef. Horseradish sauce and gravy

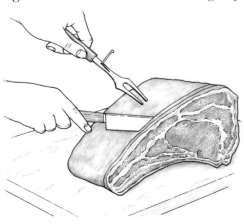

2 Carve the meat downwards, on to and between the rib bones

made from the pan juices are traditional accompaniments for a prime roast of beef, along with Yorkshire pudding (see page 15) and a selection of vegetables. Bearnaise sauce or *maitre d'hotel* butter are often-served elegant accompaniments for steaks. Other accompaniments for beef will be found throughout this book, from the 'scones' on top of a beef cobbler to the rosti potatoes often served with Steak Diane (itself a recipe including another popular accompaniment, Worcestershire sauce).

STORING BEEF

Like all meats, beef must be carefully stored to prevent it spoiling. Meat retailers have developed excellent ways of packing and storing meat to ensure it remains in peak condition for the customer, so once beef has been bought it is not difficult for the customer to keep it well, too.

Fresh beef should be stored in the coldest part of the refrigerator as soon as possible after purchase. If the beef is in a supermarket covered tray (usually made of polystyrene or fibre), it may be stored as it is. If it has been brought home in a butcher's polythene bag, it must be taken out of the bag and wrapped in clingfilm before it is put in the refrigerator.

The recommended maximum storage times for uncooked beef in a refrigerator is 3–5 days.

Cooked meats should also be wrapped carefully in clingfilm or kitchen foil before being put in the refrigerator. Storage times in the refrigerator for cooked meats are: casseroles containing bacon, 2 days; casseroles without bacon, 3 days; meat pies, 1 day; sliced beef with or without gravy, 2–3 days; beef stock 4 days.

Freezing Beef

Beef freezes well, keeping its original quality longer in the freezer than pork or lamb. Always check when buying meat for freezing that it is fresh, and not something that has been bought in ready frozen by the butcher and then thawed out before being cut up to sell. Joints and cuts can also be bought ready frozen from the butcher or supermarket to transfer to your own freezer; it is cheaper to buy part of a carcase and have it cut up and then prepared to go straight into your freezer, rather than buying odd joints here and there.

If you freeze your own beef, make sure it is very securely wrapped in freezer-weight polythene or foil, checking that there are no tears in the wrapping. If there are sharp bones or protrusions first pad these with a piece of foil before wrapping. Make sure all the air has been excluded from the pack, then, if possible, overwrap with polythene and label clearly. Meat keeps longer than any fat which may be on the joint, so it is wise to remove any excess fat or lumps of fat attached to the meat.

Beef will keep well in the freezer for up to a year in joints; steaks are best used within 6–8 months (and should be separated with strips of freezer film before packing); minced beef should be stored frozen for only 2–3 months and in usable amounts.

Cooked beef dishes will freeze for up to 2 months before beginning to deteriorate in flavour, although they are still perfectly safe to eat for several months longer. Very strongly flavoured dishes containing large amounts of onions, garlic, or spices are best used within a month. It is not advisable to freeze raw salted or pickled beef.

BUYING BEEF

British beef is available in a great variety of cuts and joints all year round, though it is most abundant in autumn (when it may also be cheaper, making autumn a good time to look for beef for filling the freezer). Whether bought from a butcher or supermarket, it should have been hung long enough to ensure optimum flavour and tenderness.

A really light, bright red colour may indicate that the beef has been insufficiently hung, but since well-hung, perfectly fresh beef can come in a variety of shades from bright red to dark red-brown, this is not much help to an inexperienced meat buyer. Shop regularly in the same butcher's shop or supermarket in order to get to know their beef and how they cut, prepare and package it.

Different colours in lean beef on a serving counter indicate only that one piece may have been cut longer than another. A short time after cutting, the pigment in beef oxidises to a bright red and then becomes browner. These colour variations do not affect the beef's eating quality and, of course, they disappear in cooking.

Whether you choose meat 'marbled' with fat (that is, with tiny particles of intramuscular fat) or very lean meat is just a matter of preference, since there is no foundation for the belief that marbled beef has a better flavour.

Many different ways of jointing and preparing beef, and also of naming joints and cuts, may be encountered in Britain. These regional variations, which grew up to suit local needs and occupations, have a long tradition. The chart below gives a selection of the most common names still used by butchers and meat retailers in Britain.

CHART OF REGIONAL NAMES FOR BEEF

WEST OF ENGLAND	WALES	N.W. ENGLAND	W. SCOTLAND	E. SCOTLAND	N.E. ENGLAND	MIDLANDS	S. EAST AND LONDON
Shin	Shin	Shin	Hough or Skink	Hough or Skink	Shin	Shin	Shin
Leg	Shin	Leg	Hough or Skink	Hough or Skink	Leg	Leg	Leg
Thick flank	Thick flank	Thick flank or First cutting	Fleshy end or Flesh end	Fleshy end or Flesh end	Thick flank or Rump top	Bed	Top rump
Steak piece Pin bone or Rump	Pin bone	Rump	Pope's eye	Henk bone	Rump or Steak bone	Hip bone or Rump	Rump
Clod	Clod	Vein	Gullet	Lyne	Sloat	Bosum	Clod
Fore rib	Fore rib	Standing	Rib roast	Rib roast	Fine chine	Chine	Fore rib

CHOOSING and COOKING *LAMB*

*B*ritain is one of the world's great producers of lamb – certainly the largest in western Europe. It is very good quality lamb, its delicate and delicious flavour helping to make it the chef's favourite meat. On both sides of the Channel restaurateurs choose lamb for their choicest menus. In France, as in Scotland, the name for a leg of lamb is 'gigot' – a reminder of the once close alliance between the two countries – and it is a favourite meal for many Frenchmen, perhaps with garlic added to enhance its flavour (but not mint sauce, the traditional British accompaniment for lamb the French do not appreciate). Since lamb is quick to cook and is available in smaller joints, ideal for one or two, it is also a favourite convenience meat in Britain.

Figures suggest we are eating more lamb than we were a few years ago, probably because it is being produced in cuts more suited to present-day social trends. This is not to say that cuts used for generations – shoulders and legs, cutlets and chops, all usually on the bone – which form the basis of so many traditional recipes are disappearing. Rather, new techniques of producing and cutting lamb have added to the range of meat available to the consumer. Nor is it a hindrance to sales that British-produced lamb is actually cheaper, even allowing for inflation, than it was in the early 1970s.

Today's lamb is leaner than ever. New cutting methods, many of them adopted from cuts used across the Channel, have produced an attractive range of trimmed and rolled cuts which can be further cut into easy-to-carve joints of any size or into boneless chops and steaks which are simple and easy to cook.

Among increasingly popular new cuts of lamb are leg steaks, boneless loin steaks, lean cubes, 'butterfly' chops, boneless breasts and even lean mince, ideal for shepherd's pie, moussaka and meatballs. Many of the boneless cuts are also delicious served 'en croûte', like beef.

These are all ideal for cooking by such quick methods as grilling, barbecuing and stir-frying because they are both lean and succulently tender.

Like all meat, lamb is an important source of protein. It also contains iron, zinc, phosphorous and B-group vitamins, making it an excellent addition to any carefully planned, well-balanced diet.

Its average fat content is higher than that of beef, though the calorie count of a lamb dish will depend on the cut of meat used and the way it has been cooked. For example, a grilled chop would contain about 222 calories per 100 g, a roast leg (a mixture of lean and fat meat) about 190 calories per 100 g and stewed scrag end piece approximately 290 calories per 100 g.

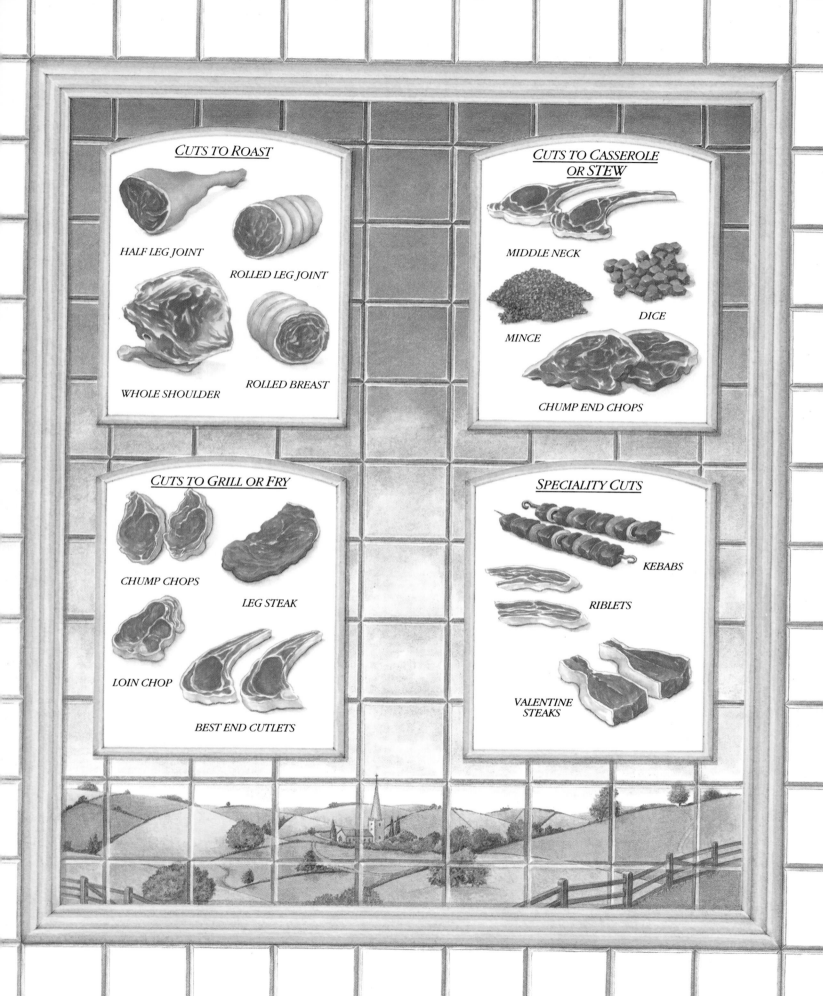

CUTS TO ROAST

HALF LEG JOINT

ROLLED LEG JOINT

WHOLE SHOULDER

ROLLED BREAST

CUTS TO CASSEROLE OR STEW

MIDDLE NECK

MINCE

DICE

CHUMP END CHOPS

CUTS TO GRILL OR FRY

CHUMP CHOPS

LEG STEAK

LOIN CHOP

BEST END CUTLETS

SPECIALITY CUTS

KEBABS

RIBLETS

VALENTINE STEAKS

HOW TO COOK LAMB

Lamb is such a tender meat that all cuts, except neck (or scrag), can be roasted successfully and slices, steaks or chops from larger cuts can be grilled or fried. It is an ideal meat for barbecuing.

Roasting

A lamb joint for roasting should be placed in a shallow tin, preferably on a grid so it does not sit in the fat and pan juices which will run off during cooking, and put into a pre-heated oven (see chart below). Unless the joint is very lean, or is being cooked in foil or a roasting bag, it should not need basting during cooking. For those who like to enhance lamb's delicate flavour, try sprinkling on the raw joint fresh herbs, especially thyme, marjoram or rosemary; lemon juice and finely grated lemon rind; or cardamom and chopped nuts. Slivers of garlic, inserted into small cuts in the joint's surface, are also used.

If a meat thermometer is used to check if the joint is cooked, a temperature of 80°C/175°F indicates it is well done; 75°C/170°F indicates medium cooked lamb.

For *spit-roasting* in specially adapted ovens, allow 15 minutes per 450 g/1 lb, plus 15 minutes, at 180°C, 350°F, Gas Mark 4.

SADDLE OR DOUBLE LOIN Large roasting joint on the bone for a special occasion. It is the whole loin from both sides of the animal with just the breast trimmed off. It is often decorated with the kidneys.

LOIN AND CHUMP The whole loin; can be roasted on the bone or boned and rolled, as can the chump. Very succulent but not over-large joints. Rack of lamb in one side of the loin cut to required size so each portion has 2–3 bones each.

LEG Prime roasting joint which is very lean. Either on the bone or boned and rolled. Can be divided into two smaller joints – fillet end and shank end.

SHOULDER A succulent, tender roasting joint, either on the bone or off. Very good to stuff and roll. Sold whole or halved into blade and knuckle end, both ideal to roast for a small number of people. Can also be pot roasted. A specially stuffed and rolled shoulder, called a 'melon', which cuts like a cake, is now available.

BREAST When boned and rolled with excess fat removed this makes a very tasty and tender joint. Many types of stuffing can be added to this extremely economical joint.

BEST END OF NECK (or RACK OF LAMB) A prime roasting joint made up of a row of 6 or 7 rib bones. Left whole, two best ends are used for the speciality joints, guard of honour and crown roast.

Pot Roasting

With this method, the pot in which the meat is quite closely confined (though it should not touch the sides) becomes the 'oven' in which the pre-browned joint is steamed in its own moisture. Most pot roasts are cooked in the oven, at a moderate temperature (180°C, 350°F, Gas Mark 4), which will allow the meat to simmer gently without sticking. The lid should only be removed when the joint is turned. All lamb cuts are suitable for pot roasting.

Braising, Stewing or Casseroling

In these slow, moist methods of cooking in a covered pot, lamb cooks more quickly than beef or pork, needing only 1½–2½ hours to the 3–4 hours of beef, depending on the cut being cooked. Lamb may be cooked by these methods in the oven (at a temperature of about 160°C, 325°F, Gas Mark 3) or simmered very gently on the stove.

As with beef cooked in this way, lamb stew or casserole or braised lamb all benefit from the addition of vegetables and herbs to give added flavour and food value. Browning the meat first also enhances flavour.

For a white stew, the traditional Irish stew, neither the meat nor the vegetables are browned before the cooking liquid is added.

CHUMP END CHOPS At the end of the chump; these uneven-shaped chops are very meaty and ideal to casserole, stew or braise.

MIDDLE NECK This is a cheaper cut with an excellent flavour. Excess fat can be removed, especially when the joint is cut into chops for stews and casseroles. It is the traditional cut for Irish Stew and Lancashire Hot Pot.

DICED LAMB Usually taken from the shoulder meat. Excess fat is discarded and the meat is cut into cubes or strips. May be sold as it is, or mixed with one of the flavourings such as Chinese, stir-fry, or barbecue, which are becoming increasingly popular.

Boiling

It is generally only mutton – which is very

ROASTING TIMES FOR LAMB		
TYPE OF JOINT	SLOW METHOD Moderately hot oven (180°C/350°F, Gas Mark 4)	FAST METHOD Hot oven (220°C/425°F, Gas Mark 7)
Meat on the bone	30–35 mins per 450 g/1 lb (depending on the thickness of the joint)	20 mins per 450 g/1 lb plus 20 mins
Meat, boned and rolled	40–45 mins per 450 g/1 lb (depending on the thickness of the joint)	25 mins per 450 g/1 lb plus 25 mins

difficult to buy retail in Britain – which is boiled, that is simmered gently in liquid. Traditional accompaniments for boiled mutton are onion or caper sauces.

Grilling, Frying and Barbecuing

When it comes to preparing quick meals with a minimum of fuss, lamb and the grill make an ideal combination. Always pre-heat the grill, and brush very lean cuts, such as leg steaks and kebabs, which have virtually no fat, with a little oil before cooking. Alternatively, a soaking in a marinade to which 1–2 tablespoons of oil have been added, is a good idea. Turn the lamb just once during grilling.

As with other meats, cooking times for grilled lamb will vary according to the thickness of the cut and how well done the lamb is preferred.

Smear oil round the pan to prevent the meat burning when frying. Fry lamb over a gentle heat at first, increasing the heat a little to brown the meat. If fat does emerge from the meat during frying, pour off the excess. When frying off mince or diced lamb before making a stew or casserole, there is no need to add extra fat to the pan.

When barbecuing, chops and cuts with a layer of fat need no extra fat, but kebabs and leg steaks, which are more likely to dry out during barbecuing, should be brushed lightly with oil or a fairly heavy marinade during cooking. Lamb riblets need no fat. Whole shoulders and legs also barbecue very well.

CHUMP CHOPS The largest of the chops, recognisable by the small round bone in the centre of each. They are cut to the thickness required.

LOIN CHOPS 'Traditional' shaped chops with a good eye of meat and tail of meat and fat which curls round it. When boned and rolled they are called 'noisettes'. Double loin chops, or 'butterfly' chops, are cut from across both loins before they have been split down the centre to give a much larger and succulent chop.

LEG AND SHOULDER STEAKS The joints are boned and then cut into steaks of varying sizes and thicknesses which may be grilled, fried or casseroled. They can be beaten to make them thinner to use for 'olives' or paupiettes or cut into strips for stir-fries and stroganoff-type dishes.

BEST END CUTLETS The best end joint is often cut into individual cutlets with one rib bone each. They may then be left as they are or, for extreme elegance, have most of the fat and lean trimmed from the bone just to leave the 'eye' of the meat to cook.

Speciality Lamb

Lamb offers an interesting array of special cuts, suitable for cooking in various ways. Some, such as guard of honour and crown roast, are ideal as the basis for impressive dinner party dishes. Others are quick and simple to cook and ideal for one-pot meals.

KEBABS Boned leg of lamb or neck fillet are cut into cubes to make kebabs which can be marinated and then grilled or barbecued.

RIBLETS These are made from breasts of lamb which have been trimmed of excess fat and cut into individual ribs to grill or barbecue.

MINCED LAMB Ideal for meatballs, burgers, pasties, pies etc.

GUARD OF HONOUR Made from two best ends of neck put facing each other, fat side outwards and the bone tips interlaced. This joint can be stuffed. It is served with the bone tips topped with cutlet frills.

CROWN OF LAMB A spectacular joint to roast made from two best ends of neck joined together and curved with the bones facing outwards. The centre of the crown is filled with stuffing and then roasted. Again, the bone tips are topped with cutlet frills.

VALENTINE STEAKS Interesting boneless steaks to fry or grill.

COOKING LAMB IN THE MICROWAVE

Lamb will cook well in the microwave cooker, provided the basic rules of microwaving are followed. In the chart below, the times were tested on a 650–700 watt cooker. Use the table as a guide, but always check with your own cooker's handbook. For cookers with a lower wattage, add a few minutes to the times in the chart.

Cut	Time for 450 g/1 lb	Standing Time	Special Points
Leg–on the bone	11 mins	25–30 mins	Use 70% power.
Leg–off the bone	11 mins	25–30 mins	Use 70% power.
Crown roast (stuffed)	11 mins	15 mins	Protect bone tips with foil, use 70% power.
Loin lamb	11 mins	15 mins	Use 70% power.
Chops loin chump cutlets (best end)	8 mins		Use browning dish and 100% power.

TRADITIONAL ROAST LAMB

*approx 1.75 kg/4 lb prime roasting joint
  of lamb – leg, shoulder or double loin*
salt and black pepper
crushed garlic (optional)
fresh or dried rosemary (optional)

Accompaniments
Mint sauce (see below)
redcurrant jelly
*Onion sauce (generally served with
  mutton) (See below)*
gravy
roast potatoes
garden peas

Trim the meat if necessary and weigh it.
Calculate the cooking time and oven
temperature from the chart on page 20,
deciding whether you want to cook it by
the cooler or hot method.

Stand the joint in a roasting tin with
the thickest layer of fat upwards and
season with a little salt and pepper, if
liked. The surface may be rubbed all
over with a crushed clove of garlic and
sprinkled or rubbed with fresh or dried
rosemary.

Roast for the calculated cooking time
(see chart on page 20), basting the joint
several times, as the juices run from the
joint. Potatoes may be roasted around it
for the last hour of cooking time.

When cooked, remove to a serving
dish and allow to stand and set for 10
minutes or so.

Spoon the excess fat from the pan
juices and use the juices with stock to
make a gravy. Serve with mint
sauce and/or redcurrant jelly or, if
preferred, a rich onion sauce.

SERVES 6

MINT SAUCE

about 8 large sprigs of fresh mint
1 tablespoon caster sugar
1 tablespoon boiling water
2–3 tablespoons vinegar

Wash and dry the mint leaves well and
then strip from the stalks and chop finely.
Dissolve the sugar in the boiling water,
add the chopped mint and vinegar to
taste. This sauce can be made in larger
quantities and stored in an airtight container
in the refrigerator for up to 10 days.

RICH ONION SAUCE

40 g/1½ oz butter or margarine
*175 g/6 oz onions, peeled and finely
  chopped*
40 g/1½ oz plain flour
450 ml/¾ pint milk or milk and stock
good dash of Worcestershire sauce
salt and black pepper

Melt the fat in a pan and fry the onions
very gently until soft, but not coloured,
stirring frequently. Stir in the flour and
cook for a minute or so and then

A traditional lamb roast: Stuffed Guard of Honour (see page 133 for recipe)

gradually add the milk and bring slowly to the boil. Add the Worcestershire sauce and seasonings and simmer for 5–10 minutes, very gently.

AVERAGE AMOUNTS OF LAMB TO ALLOW	
TYPES OF MEAT	AMOUNTS PER PERSON
Joints on the bone	350 g/12 oz per portion, but allowing a little more for loin and best end joints, plus some extra to serve cold.
Boned and rolled joints	175–225 g/6–9 oz per portion before adding any stuffing, and allowing a little more if stuffing is not used, plus extra to serve cold.
Stewing lamb; breast of lamb	225–350 g/8–12 oz per portion.
Chops	1 or 2, depending on size.
Cutlets	at least 2.
Double loin chops	1, unless very small.
Chump chops	1.
Steaks and other cuts	1 or 2, depending on size.

CARVING AND SERVING LAMB

Follow the general rules for carving beef (see page 16). Stand the joint neatly and squarely on a board or large plate and allow it to 'set' for several minutes before beginning to carve.

Lamb should not be carved too thinly; try to aim for about 5 mm/¼ inch thick. With loin and best end of neck joints on the bone, ask the butcher to chine the joint first, which means he will partly chop through the backbone lengthwise so the bone can be removed before carving to make it easier to carve between the rib bones. If the bone were removed before cooking the meat would shrink from the bones and look unattractive.

Alternatively, the joint can be chopped in such a way that every bone or every other one is only partly chopped through so when it is cooked it just needs the cut completing – chopping does not give such a good looking cooked joint and may cause it to overcook in places.

Bone-In Joints

LEG Stand with the meatier side of the leg uppermost and the carving fork firmly embedded in the knuckle end. Carve a narrow wedge-shaped piece of meat from the middle of the leg, right down to the bone. Now carve slices from either side of this first cut, slanting the knife to obtain larger slices. The underside of the joint can be carved, after removing any excess fat, by slicing along the length of the leg.

SADDLE Stand on a board and begin by making a cut across the joint at the end of the loin to the bone and then a cut along the backbone (see photograph, pages 98–9). Run the knife between the meat and bone, lift off the meat and carve in slices. Leave the base of the saddle on the bone and carve in horizontal slices from it.

SHOULDER This is the most difficult joint to carve. To simplify carving you can loosen around the blade bone in the raw joint with a small sharp knife, but do not

Carving a shoulder

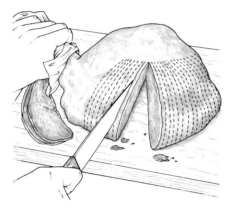

1 Cut along the bone to release parallel cuts

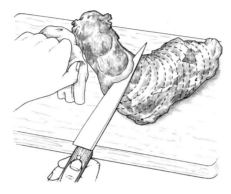

2 Carve horizontal slices from the underside

Carving a leg

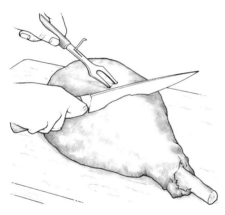

1 First, carve a wedge-shaped slice from the middle of the leg on the meatiest side

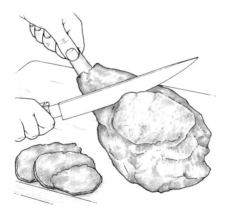

2 For the underside, carve in long horizontal slices

remove it. When cooked this can be loosened and then pulled out to make carving easier. Hold the joint at the shank end, with the crisp skin uppermost. Cut a wedge-shaped slice through the middle of the joint in the angle between the shoulder blade and the arm bone. Carve slices from each side of the first cut until the shoulder blade and arm bone are reached. Turn the joint over and carve horizontal slices from underneath the joint. Take care with horizontal slices that the fork guard is in position to prevent cuts if the knife should slip.

BEST END OF NECK Stand the chined joint squarely on a plate and remove the backbone with a sharp knife. Carve between the ribs to divide the joint neatly into cutlets. If the joint is from a particularly large animal, some slices may have no bone. The joint can also be cut into portions rather than slices to give each person a 'mini' joint of 2 or 3 bones, if preferred.

BONED AND ROLLED JOINTS Remove skewers and string as necessary and carve into slices, not too thinly, standing the joint firmly on a plate so it will not slip.

Lamb is traditionally served well done, but can be served slightly pink in the centre; but definitely not rare.

The traditional accompaniments to roast lamb are mint sauce, redcurrant jelly and gravy. Roast mutton is served with onion sauce and boiled mutton with caper sauce. Roast potatoes are cooked alongside the joint and the traditional favourite vegetable accompaniment was – and still is – fresh garden peas.

However, other types of potatoes, such as baked jacket potatoes, new potatoes Lyonnaise or scalloped potatoes are all excellent choices. Any green vegetable goes well with lamb, as do carrot sticks with parsley or sugar glaze, roasted parsnips, leeks, ratatouille, braised fennel, marrow or courgettes – to suggest just a few.

STORING LAMB

Fresh lamb or mutton may be stored in the refrigerator for 3–5 days only. Raw lamb, including joints and chops bought from a butcher and put into a polythene bag by him, should be put on a plate and left uncovered, or be loosely covered with greaseproof paper or tightly wrapped in clingfilm. Supermarket lamb bought in covered trays can be stored as it is still in the trays. Raw minced lamb should only be stored for 24 hours before use.

Cooked dishes should be cooled quickly, covered with clingfilm and stored in the coldest part of the refrigerator for up to 2 days. Cooked joints should be treated the same way.

Freezing Lamb

Lamb is an excellent meat to freeze for the carcase is not too large to fit into most freezers and you can buy a whole or half carcase or sometimes a hindquarter (leg and loin) or forequarter (shoulder, neck, best end and breast), or individual joints, chops etc to suit the requirements of your family.

The butcher will cut up a whole or half carcase to your requirements, provided you ask him in advance, and often it will come ready packaged. It is very important that the lamb is very securely wrapped in freezer-weight foil or polythene, making sure there are no tears in the wrapping; pad any sharp bones or protrusions before wrapping, with extra foil or polythene. Make sure all the air is excluded and if in any doubt or if you do not have special freezer weight wrappings, overwrap with a polythene bag. It is wise to separate chops with freezer film before packaging so they can be removed singly, if required. 'Freezer burn', which is an unsightly greyish-white patch caused by exposure to the freezing temperature, is, in fact, harmless but it affects the flavour and texture of the lamb. Remember to label clearly with cut and date and keep a record of what you put into the freezer. Recommended storage times are 9–12 months for raw lamb and mutton, with chops better if used within the shorter time.

It is best thoroughly to thaw all lamb joints and cuts before cooking for the best results; however chops and cubes can be started from frozen in a casserole or hotpot, increasing the cooking time by 30–45 minutes. Grilling and frying can also be done from frozen with care and allowing longer cooking times. Boned and rolled joints must always be thawed first because of the depth of the meat; bone-in joints can be cooked from frozen but you must use a meat thermometer for guidance as to when the meat is properly cooked.

Lamb can be thawed in a microwave (see manufacturers' recommended times) or be left at room temperature when joints will take approx. 6–7 hours per 450 g/1 lb for larger joints or a little less for small joints under 1.5 kg/3.3 lb.

Cooked dishes will freeze well for up to 2 months unless they are highly spiced or very full of onions and garlic when it is advisable to store for only 4–6 weeks. Always cover and package very well before freezing. Frozen lamb once cooked may then be frozen quite safely. However, do not refreeze cooked dishes once thawed; always recook and eat.

BUYING LAMB

When buying lamb look for fine grained lean meat. The flesh should be pinkish-brown and this darkens as the season progresses and turns to a light red when it becomes mutton. The fat should be white or creamy white but not yellow. The colour of the flesh or fat does not indicate the eating quality, only age, and these colour variations disappear on cooking.

Mutton, which used to be so popular in Britain and one of our traditional dishes, is now hard to find.

The best of the British lamb is new season or spring lamb. The meat is delicate and widely sought after. As it is not all that plentiful, prices may be higher. As the season progresses, lamb becomes more plentiful and prices begin to drop. For bulk-buying of a whole or half carcase for the freezer the best time is late summer and autumn when prices are usually at their lowest and the quality is still excellent. The peak months for buying lamb are between August and November. New spring lamb appears in March.

The chart below gives regional names applied to different joints and cuts of lamb in Britain.

CHART OF REGIONAL NAMES FOR LAMB							
WEST OF ENGLAND	WALES	N.W. ENGLAND	W. SCOTLAND	E. SCOTLAND	N.E. ENGLAND	MIDLANDS	S. EAST AND LONDON
Fillet Knuckle	Shank	Fillet Shank	Gigot	Gigot	Fillet Shank	Fillet Knuckle	Leg-fillet Knuckle
Chump chops	Chump	Gigot chops	Chump chops	Chump chops	Gigot chops	Leg chops	Chump chops
Best end of neck	Best end of neck	Fine end Loin	Loin or single loin	Loin or single loin	Fine end Loin	Cutlets	Best end of neck
Breast	Breast	Lap	Flank	Flank	Lap	Breast	Breast

CHOOSING
and
COOKING
PORK
and BACON

*B*ritons today are eating more pork than ever – partly because there is more choice than ever before. Pork is leaner than ever, and there are many new cuts available. Bacon, too, is available in a greater variety of ways – steaks, small boneless joints and others. Vacuum packing also means that bacon will keep much longer – up to 15 days in the refrigerator.

Most pork sold in Britain is also produced here, with only a small percentage coming from Denmark.

Although we are still very fond of our traditional roast Sunday joint, its rind cooked to a delicious crisp crackling, served with apple sauce, and of our sausages, bacon and pork pies, we are also eating many new, lean cuts of British pork.

Compact, evenly shaped boneless joints are now produced which are easy to carve and serve. There is also a splendid variety of lean, virtually fat-free boneless cuts and steaks – topside leg, shoulder and double loin – ideal for cooking by such quick methods as grilling, frying, barbecuing or stir-frying or, when minced, for turning into burgers, meatballs and meat sauces.

Bacon is pork which has been preserved or cured. Most of this is then sold either as it is as 'green' bacon or, after smoking, as 'smoked' bacon. A small quantity is given other specialist or sweet cures to provide bacon with unusual flavours.

There are several ways of curing bacon, the most popular of which is the 'Wiltshire' cure, a process which takes about 10 days. Green bacon has a pale rind and deep pink flesh, and the most popular variety of smoked bacon has a deep golden brown rind and brownish red lean.

Like beef and lamb, pork is a good source of high quality protein, along with vitamins B12, B1 (or thiamin, of which pork is a particularly rich source), riboflavin, and niacin and important minerals. Today's pork is much leaner, with an average fat content of 5 g per 100 g of lean meat. If fat is a problem in your diet, it is easy to trim off the visible fat before or after cooking.

The energy (calories) we obtain from pork varies with the amount of visible fat. For pork leg, lean only, a 100 g portion gives 185 calories. The lean part of a grilled loin chop gives 185 calories per 100 g.

With bacon, boiled collar joint, lean only, gives 191 calories, while boiled gammon, lean only, gives 167 calories per 100 g portion. Grilled back rashers, lean only, give 290 calories per 100 g portion.

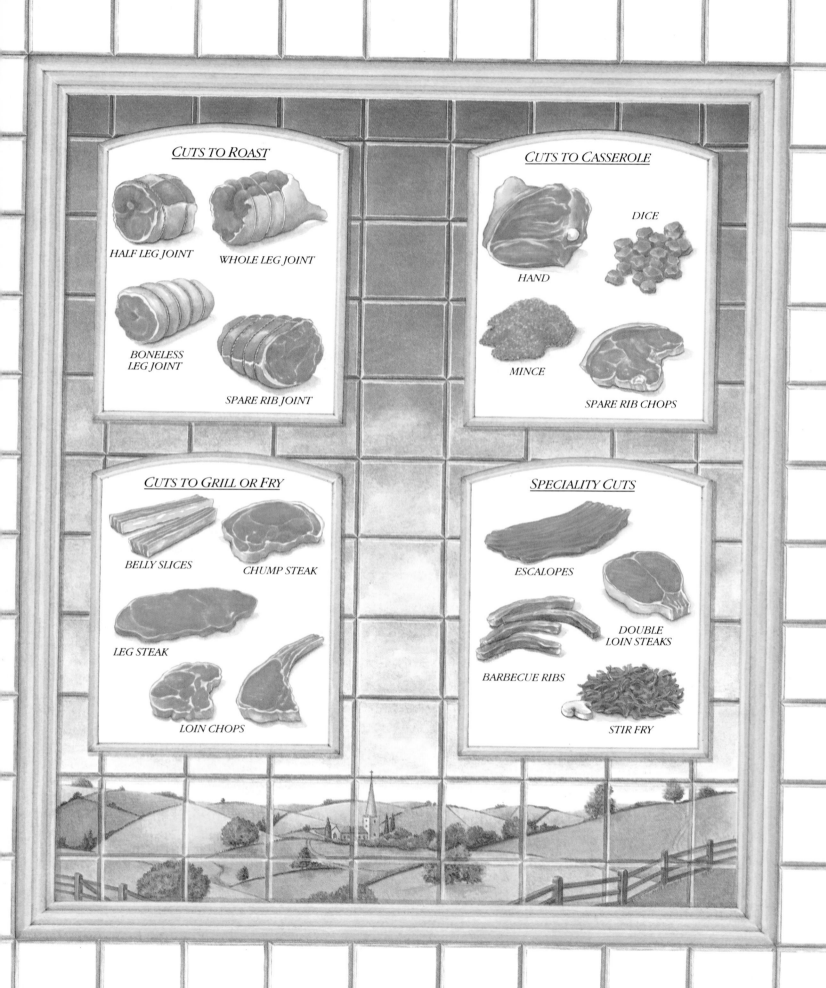

CUTS TO ROAST

HALF LEG JOINT

WHOLE LEG JOINT

BONELESS
LEG JOINT

SPARE RIB JOINT

CUTS TO CASSEROLE

HAND

DICE

MINCE

SPARE RIB CHOPS

CUTS TO GRILL OR FRY

BELLY SLICES

CHUMP STEAK

LEG STEAK

LOIN CHOPS

SPECIALITY CUTS

ESCALOPES

DOUBLE
LOIN STEAKS

BARBECUE RIBS

STIR FRY

HOW TO COOK PORK AND BACON

Pork is a good all-purpose meat which, depending on the cut, is suitable for all kinds of cooking, including microwaving.

Cooking Crackling

Most people like pork crackling, but all the cuts of pork can be prepared with the rind off, if preferred. For good crackling, ask the butcher to score the rind evenly either into narrow strips or a criss-cross; prepackaged joints should be ready scored. Dry and then brush the cut surface with oil or melted lard and rub a good layer of salt into it. Put the joint in a dry roasting tin or on a rack in a tin and do not baste, or only baste lightly once during cooking. The rind on chops will crackle when crisply grilled; but for moist methods of cooking it is best to remove the skin as it will not crisp into crackling.

Roasting

Just about all cuts of pork can be roasted. The joint to be roasted should be placed in a shallow pan, preferably on a grid, and put in a preheated oven. For temperatures and cooking times, see the chart below.

Unless the joint is very lean, it should not need basting. Lean, rindless meat should be brushed lightly with oil before being put in the oven and basted frequently during cooking.

Pork must be well cooked, and never served 'rare', so a meat thermometer, pushed right into the centre of the joint, is particularly useful with pork; a temperature of 85°C/185°F indicates the pork is well done.

For *spit-roasting*, use the same oven temperature as for roasting, allowing about half the cooking time per 450 g/1 lb.

LEG This is a large joint which can be roasted whole but is more often cut into up to four roasting joints. The fillet end (the thick end) can be divided into smaller joints, and is the prime roasting joint to cook on or off the bone, as it is or stuffed. The whole leg is often boned out and rolled and then the required amount cut off. The knuckle or shank end is good for roasting with lots of crackling.

SPARE RIB This joint comes from the shoulder and can be a large joint when combined with the blade bone. It is very good when boned and rolled. The two smaller cuts can also be roasted or cooked in other ways. It is fairly lean and the flavour is excellent. Blade or shoulder of pork is less fatty.

BELLY Although thought to be fatty, this need not be so, and when carefully boned, excess fat removed and rolled up with stuffing, it makes a very good and extremely economical roasting joint to serve hot or cold.

HAND AND SPRING This is the foreleg of the pig and is a large roasting joint. Can be divided up into smaller joints for roasting. It is relatively inexpensive, fairly lean and very well flavoured. It is one of the most versatile of the pork joints.

LOIN A favourite smaller joint of pork. It can be roasted on or off the bone, and with or without the kidney. Good crackling makes this a good joint for a not too large family. Ask the butcher to chop or chine the loin before you cook it, to make carving easier.

Boiling

This cooking method is recommended for salt pork. The meat should be first soaked for several hours, preferably overnight, before being drained and put into fresh cold water to cover, with vegetables for flavouring, in a pan with a securely fitting lid.

The water should simmer, not boil, which would make the meat tough. For large joints, allow 25 minutes per 450 g/1 lb and for smaller joints a minimum of 1½ hours.

Braising, Stewing and Casseroling

These methods can be done on top of the stove or in the oven. For stewing or casseroling, cook in the oven at a temperature of 160°C, 325°F, Gas Mark 3, or on top of the stove at a heat which allows the contents of the casserole to simmer gently but not boil. Cooking times will vary, depending on the quality of the meat, but allow about 2–3 hours.

For braising a joint, allow 45 minutes per 450 g/1 lb; in the oven, braise at 180°C, 350°F, Gas Mark 4.

HAND A lean part of the pig – the foreleg which is ideal to cut into dice or to mince for a variety of stews and casserole. Tender cut which needs only about an hour to cook, do not overcook or the texture will be spoilt.

SPARE RIB When cut into chops these make an excellent casserole and can be braised equally well. Very little fat and very tasty meat.

BLADE BONE Sometimes called shoulder of pork, this is ideal to cube, cut into individual portions or mince to create many different dishes.

ROASTING TIMES FOR PORK		
Pork on the bone	Hot oven (220°C/425°F, Gas Mark 7)	25–30 mins per 450 g/1 lb plus 25 mins (depending on the thickness of the joint)
Pork, boned and	Moderately hot oven (190°C/375°F, Gas Mark 5)	30–35 mins per 450 g/1 lb plus 30 mins (depending on the thickness of the joint)

Grilling, Frying and Barbecuing

Always preheat the grill. If the pork or bacon is very lean, brush it with a little oil before putting it under the grill. Turn the meat during cooking. Cooking times will vary according to the thickness of the cut, but make sure the meat is cooked right through and is not pink.

Frying can be done in very little oil if a non-stick pan is used. Smear the pan with a little oil and turn the chop or steak once during cooking. No extra fat is needed when barbecuing, for which pork is ideal, but the cuts can be made extra-delicious by marinating them before cooking, with extra oil added if the cut is very lean.

LOIN CHOPS Good chops with an even layer of fat, some with slices of kidney attached. Also available boned as pork slices or steaks. Grill, fry or barbecue.

CHUMP CHOPS Larger and meatier than loin chops with only an 'eye' of bone. Can also be pan fried or braised.

BELLY A long, thin cut with streaks of fat and lean; full of flavour and economical. When boned and cut into slices it is ideal to fry, grill or barbecue. It can also be braised, but it needs to be cooked the day before, so the layer of fat produced can be removed.

LEG STEAKS Slices taken from the boned-out leg are lean and are ready to cook in a variety of ways. If grilling, take care not to let them dry out.

FILLET OR TENDERLOIN A prime piece of meat with no fat on it. Found just underneath the back bone, it is the equivalent of beef fillet. Do not confuse with the fillet end of the leg. It is most versatile and can be cooked whole, in slices, for kebabs etc. Must be kept moist as it has no fat of its own. Pan frying in slices is one of the best cooking methods.

Speciality cuts

New techniques of boning a whole side of pork have produced new cuts and made other joints and cuts more widely available.

ESCALOPES These slices of very lean meat are cut with the grain so they are extra tender. Can be beaten out to make even thinner. Can be used in the same ways as veal escalopes.

BARBECUE RIBS Sometimes called American spare ribs, these are slices from the belly and trimmed of most of the flesh. Ideal to grill or cook on a barbecue either with or without marinating.

DOUBLE LOIN STEAK A large steak with a thin edging of fat.

STIR FRY Strips of pork from the hand and blade cut into varying size pieces to sell as they are, or ready mixed with one of the spiced preparations now available.

CROWN OF PORK Similar to a crown of lamb, but larger. The skin and some fat are removed before joining the two loins together.

KEBAB Ready skewered by the butcher, with or without vegetables, ready to grill or barbecue.

COOKING PORK AND BACON IN THE MICROWAVE

Microwaving is a quick and easy way of cooking pork and bacon and the results are delicious, provided the basic rules of microwaving are followed. The times below were tested on a 650–700 watt cooker. Use this table as a guide, but always check with your own cooker's handbook as well. For cookers with a lower wattage add a few minutes.

CUT	TIME FOR 450 g/1 lb	STANDING TIME	SPECIAL POINTS
Leg fillet end	12 mins	30 mins	Remove crackling and crisp separately under a hot grill. Use 70% power.
Knuckle	12 mins	30 mins	Use 70% power.
Loin whole (boned & rolled)	12 mins	30 mins	Use 70% power.
Chops loin chump	8 mins		Turn chops once. Use browning dish and 100% power.
Pork fillet	8 mins	10 mins	Use 70% power.
Sausages	5–6 mins full power		Use browning dish. Turn once.
Gammon steaks	6 mins		Use browning dish and 100% power. Turn steaks once.
Collar joint	18 mins	30 mins	Use 50% power, cover joint when cooking. Initial 5 mins on full power.
Streaky/Back rashers	1 min per rasher		Cook on plate or kitchen paper.

Cuts of Bacon and Ham

The choice of bacon joints is wide. Gammon tends to be leaner and costs more, collar and forehock are more economical.

BACK BACON This lean cut is usually sold as rashers or boneless chops to be grilled or fried. Back bacon can be rolled into a joint with or without stuffing to boil or bake.

MIDDLE OR THROUGHCUT These are long rashers that combine the back and the streaky. It is also good to use as a joint for boiling or baking and is delicious stuffed.

STREAKY BACON These are narrow rashers from the belly which have lean and fat streaked together. The flavour is excellent. Best grilled or fried, it is also used for lining pâté dishes and chopped for casseroles, soups and rice dishes. A joint of streaky is delicious boiled.

COLLAR Taken from the shoulder, this is one of the best boiling joints when boned and rolled, for it is full of flavour. Joints vary in size from small, at about 450 g/1 lb, up to very large at 3.5 kg/8 lb or more. Boil, braise or casserole. Collar rashers are fairly substantial and basically lean with just a rim of fat.

FOREHOCK Whole hocks can be bought very cheaply with the bone still in, ready to cook. They are more often sold boned and rolled when they can be cut into any size of joint. Sometimes the forehock can be cut into two smaller joints. The flavour is very good and it is fairly lean. Boil, braise or pot-roast.

GAMMON OR HAM The most prized part of the side of bacon both for leanness and fine texture. It is often sold ready cooked either on or off the bone. Buy raw as a whole or half gammon or as smaller cuts which are known as the middle, corner and gammon hock. Most of these joints are ready boned to boil, bake or braise.

Gammon steaks and rashers are cut off this joint after it has been boned and are best grilled or fried or rolled up to braise.

Cooking Bacon Joints

Large smoked joints are best if soaked in cold water for 12–18 hours before cooking to remove some of the excess salt acquired during curing to prevent the cooked joint tasting too salty; with milder cures or green bacon joints sometimes it is unnecessary to soak at all or, if you want, just for 4–6 hours. Always discard the soak-water and cook the joint in fresh water with preferably 1–2 bay leaves, a peeled and quartered onion and 1–2 peeled and sliced carrots. 1–2 tablespoons brown sugar added to the water will help offset extra saltiness.

Always weigh the joint before cooking and calculate the time, allowing 20–25 minutes per 450 g/1 lb plus 20 minutes over for joints up to 4.5 kg/10 lb. For larger joints allow 15–20 minutes per 450 g/1 lb plus 15 minutes over. For joints to serve cold, remove the pan from the heat and leave the joint in the water for an hour or so before removing. When cold strip off the skin. To serve hot, remove from the water and carefully ease away the skin. Glaze the joint, using marmalade, honey, and/or brown sugar, cut criss-cross patterns in it and insert cloves.

AVERAGE AMOUNTS OF PORK TO ALLOW

TYPES OF MEAT	AMOUNTS PER PERSON
Joints on the bone	225–350 g/8–12 oz per portion, plus extra to serve cold.
Boned and rolled joints	about 175 g/6 oz per portion, plus extra to serve cold.
Chops	1
Cutlets, boneless pork slices	1 or 2, or about 100–175 g/4–6 oz per portion.
Hand and spring	350 g/12 oz per portion.
Tenderloin	100–175 g/4–6 oz per portion.
Belly	100–225 g/4–8 oz per portion.

AVERAGE AMOUNTS OF BACON TO ALLOW

TYPES OF MEAT	AMOUNTS PER PERSON
Bacon rashers	2–4 per portion for back and streaky; 1 for gammon; 1–2 for collar, all depending on size and what they are served with.
Bacon chops	1–2, depending on size.
Gammon steaks	1, weighing about 150–175 g/5–6 oz.
Joints on the bone	175 g/6 oz per portion, plus extra to serve cold.
Boned and rolled joints	225–350 g/8–12 oz per portion, plus extra to serve cold.

CLASSIC ROAST PORK

*1 × 1.5–1.75 kg/3–4 lb joint of loin or
    leg of pork on the bone, well scored*
salt
oil

Sage and onion stuffing
2 onions, peeled and chopped
1 tablespoon oil
100 g/4 oz fresh white breadcrumbs
2 teaspoons dried sage
salt and black pepper
1 dessert apple, peeled, cored and grated

Preheat the oven to hot (220°C, 425°F, Gas Mark 7). You should allow 25–30 minutes per 450 g/1 lb plus 25 minutes over to roast a pork joint – the longer time for a leg joint.

Wipe the joint all over, then brush the crackling with oil and rub salt thoroughly into the skin, leaving a surface of salt. Stand in a roasting tin and add about 2–3 tablespoons oil to the tin for roasting potatoes.

Cook in the preheated oven for an hour, then arrange potatoes to roast around the joint, making sure they are well coated in oil. Return to the oven for 1–1½ hours, depending on the size and thickness of the joint. It is not necessary to baste the joint but the potatoes do need basting.

Whilst the pork is cooking make the stuffing: put the onions into a pan of water, bring to the boil and boil for 5 minutes. Then drain very thoroughly. Heat the oil in a pan, add the onions and fry for a few minutes until soft but not coloured.

Put the breadcrumbs into a bowl and mix in the sage, seasonings and the apple. Add the onions and mix well.

Either press lightly into a greased ovenproof shallow dish and cook in the oven below the joint for 30–40 minutes until browned on top and crisp; or form into balls about the size of a walnut and stand on a greased baking sheet and cook below the joint for 20–25 minutes. Keep warm.

When ready to serve: remove the pork from the roasting tin and stand on a serving dish. Leave to set for 10 minutes and use the pan juices to make gravy. Arrange roast potatoes and stuffing balls around the joint and serve with apple sauce and other vegetables. If the stuffing is cooked in a dish it should be served cut into wedges.

SERVES 6

CARVING AND SERVING PORK AND BACON

Joints of both pork and ham need to be carefully carved to preserve their appearance on the plate and their eating quality.

Carving Pork

Follow the general rules for carving beef (see page 16). Stand the joint neatly and squarely on a board or large plate and allow it to 'set' before beginning.

Loin Sever the chined bone from the chop bones and set aside. It is easier to remove the crackling first before beginning to carve, but not every one likes to do this. Divide the joint into chops, cutting between the rib bones and the scored crackling (if it has not already been removed) and serve as chops. Alternatively, loosen the meat from the bones after cutting off the chined backbone and then cut off in slices without dividing into chops. Cut the crackling or break it into even-sized pieces for each portion.

Leg-shank end Remove some of the crackling to make carving easier. Cut thin slices down from the face to and around the bone. When the bone is reached, carve obliquely over the top of the bone. Turn the whole joint over and cut oblique slices downwards, towards the thin end of the bone. Keep the slices fairly thin.

Leg-fillet end Carve slices through to the bone, on either side of it.

Spare rib Cut between the score marks into fairly thick slices.

Carving Ham and Bacon

All ham and bacon should be carved thinly and the knife must be extra sharp; often a special ham knife which is long and thin is kept specially for carving ham.

Whole gammon There are several methods but the simplest is probably to remove a small slice from the knuckle end of the bone and then carve in long oblique

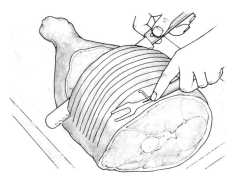

Carving a whole gammon joint

slices to the bone on either side. An alternative method is to carve slices at an angle from either side of the bone. Hold the knife at an oblique angle and cut long thin slices from each side.

Accompaniments

Apple sauce, with the option of sage and onion stuffing, roast potatoes and gravy, are the traditional accompaniments for roast pork. However, sometimes a gooseberry sauce is served in preference to apple; and the apple may be served as baked halved apples, or pan-fried apples as a garnish. The tartness of apple blends very well with pork. Vegetables which blend well with pork are all types of beans, carrots, cauliflower in white sauce, broccoli, carrots, leeks, greens or cabbage, red cabbage, baked onions, celery, courgettes or marrow, sprouts etc.

Boiled bacon is particularly good served with parsley sauce or a sage and onion sauce together with creamed potatoes and a green vegetable. Baked ham or gammon is more sophisticated and needs similar accompaniments to roast pork although baked jacket potatoes or new potatoes also go well. Don't forget to serve mustard (of some variety) with bacon or ham; some people like it with pork, too.

Cold pork or bacon are particularly good with Lyonnaise potatoes (onions fried with potatoes), sauté potatoes and jacket potatoes. Bubble and squeak also goes well, as does any type of salad.

Cumberland sauce is a traditional accompaniment for cold bacon.

STORING PORK AND BACON

As with other meats, all types of pork must be stored in refrigerator or freezer as soon as possible after it is brought home.

Fresh Pork and Bacon

Before the invention of refrigeration it was said that pork should only be eaten when there was an 'R' in the month, that is in the colder months. In fact, pork is an ideal summer meat for it is then lower in price, so a good time to buy in bulk for the freezer, and it is an ideal quick cooking meat for use on barbecues and grills.

Pork fat does go rancid more quickly than beef or lamb so should not be stored for longer than necessary, about 3–4 days in the refrigerator.

Bacon keeps longer; with smoked or unsmoked joints, rashers, chops, steaks etc keeping for up to 10 days and vacuum packs for 3 days or so longer.

Cooked Pork and Bacon

All cooked dishes should be cooled as quickly as possible and covered tightly with cling film. Cooked pork will keep for 2–3 days. Cooked bacon and ham in vacuum packs will keep for up to 5 days (keep an eye on the date stamp), loose sliced ham, for 2 days; cooked joints of ham for 5–6 days and casseroles with bacon for up to 2 days.

Freezing

Pork is a good meat to freeze, especially in the summer and early autumn when prices are usually at their lowest. Most joints will come 'bone in' and should you need any boned, or any special ways of cutting it up, you must tell the supplier well in advance to avoid disappointment.

The meat should be packaged tightly in freezer weight polythene or foil as for other types of meat. The rind should be thin and supple, the flesh fine grained and a pale pink with a creamy white firm fat. It is best to get roasting joints 'scored' before freezing, as it is not so easy to do afterwards.

The fat on pork tends to turn rancid

before other types of meat so the recommended storage times are less than for other meats; it is still safe to eat after this time but may not be quite at its peak. Do not freeze salted or pickled pork for the salt accelerates the speed at which rancidity starts. Once thawed treat as fresh meat and use accordingly.

Bacon, because it has been salted, has a shorter storage life in the freezer. Vacuum packed joints and rashers will store for longer because all the air has been extracted. It must not be packed in foil, for the salt reacts with the aluminium to cause 'pitting' and 'pin-prick holes' and this will cause freezer burn. Always package securely in freezer weight polythene and/or cling wrap.

Uncooked pork – 6 months.
Pork mince – 3 months.
Pork pâté – 1 month.
Bacon joints – up to 1 month;
    if vacuum packed up to 3 months.
Bacon rashers, chops, steaks – up
    to 1 month; if vacuum packed up to
    6 months.

Cooked pork dishes will freeze well for up to 2 months except when they contain bacon, when 1 month is sufficient.

BUYING PORK AND BACON

When buying pork, look for meat that is pale pink and firm, the lean smooth with little, if any, gristle, and the fat firm and white with a thinnish, elastic skin. A roasting joint should have a good rind that can be scored into narrow strips with a very sharp knife to give a good crackling. The butcher will prepare the crackling, if asked, and most supermarkets sell roasting joints with the rind already scored.

As there is no standard method of carcase cutting in Britain, there are many local variations to be found on labels in shops and supermarkets. The chart below is intended as a guide to the most commonly used regional names for pork cuts and joints.

New cutting techniques provide cuts which are becoming well known throughout the country. These boneless lean pork cuts have extended the range of pork available to shoppers, offering meat suitable for those on a low-fat diet and for those who want their pork in convenient, quick-to-cook forms. Thus, pork can be bought cut and trimmed ready for kebabs, stir-fry dishes, grills, barbecues and many other types of meal.

Bacon is sold both 'loose' or packaged in vacuum packs. Bacon in vacuum packs will keeper longer than loose and remain moist until opened, but then will dry and deteriorate in the same way as fresh. Both rashers and joints can be vacuum packed.

Charter Quality British bacon is the highest quality so it is well worth looking out for.

Gammon is the cured whole leg of a pig. It is called 'gammon' when eated hot, but is known as 'ham' when served cold. Ham may be sold freshly sliced or in vacuum packs.

York and Bradenham hams are examples of special hams which are removed from the carcase and cured and cooked according to the manufacturers' own recipes. Old Smokey and Virginia-style are other special cures.

CHART OF REGIONAL NAMES FOR PORK							
WEST OF ENGLAND	WALES	N.W. ENGLAND	W. SCOTLAND	E. SCOTLAND	N.E. ENGLAND	MIDLANDS	S. EAST AND LONDON
Pork chops	Pork chops	Loin or pork chops	Single loin	Double loin or Single loin	Loin or pork chops	Loin or pork chops	Loin or pork chops
Spare rib	Spare rib	Spare rib	Rolled pork and shoulder	Rolled pork and shoulder	Shoulder or spare rib	Spare rib	Spare rib
Hand	Shoulder	Shoulder	Rolled pork and shoulder	Rolled pork and shoulder	Shoulder	Shoulder	Hand and spring

CHOOSING
and
COOKING
OFFAL

Offal, or 'variety meats', is highly nutritious, tasty and economical. We could, with great advantage to our diets and our housekeeping budgets, eat much more of it than we do – and be more adventurous in our cooking of it.

Apart from calf's liver, a delicacy akin to fillet steak in price, offal is an economical buy and is also extremely nutritious. It is available all year round.

To most people, 'offal' means liver, kidneys and heart. There is, in fact, much more to offal. As well as these three favourites, offal includes tongue, sweetbreads, tripe and brain as well as trotters, oxtail, ox cheek and head.

All kinds of offal have strong or rich flavours, they have no bones, which means that smaller portions are needed than for other meats and, of course, there is no waste. It is probably the distinctive flavours which have made offal meats the basis of numerous highly prized regional delicacies in Britain, including Scotland's haggis and the black pudding found in many parts of the north of England.

Today, offal is recognized as an ideal basis for nourishing, easily digested, value-for-money meals, from slowly cooked casseroles based on oxtail or heart to quickly and easily prepared and cooked liver and kidney dishes. All offal should be eaten as fresh as possible, since it does not keep as well as other meats.

The various types of offal vary in their nutritional value; liver of all types is the most nutritious, with kidneys the next best. They are rich in haem iron, a form of iron which is absorbed most efficiently into the body. All types of liver are extremely rich in vitamin A and are a useful source of vitamin D; they also contain some vitamin C. Liver is also richer than the other meats in the B vitamins. Sweetbreads, tripe and heart are good sources of protein.

A 100 g/4 oz portion of grilled or fried liver provides about 45% of the recommended daily intake of protein, and enough iron, vitamin A and riboflavin for a day. A chart on page 38 indicates the nutrient content in a variety of other offal dishes when cooked by several different methods.

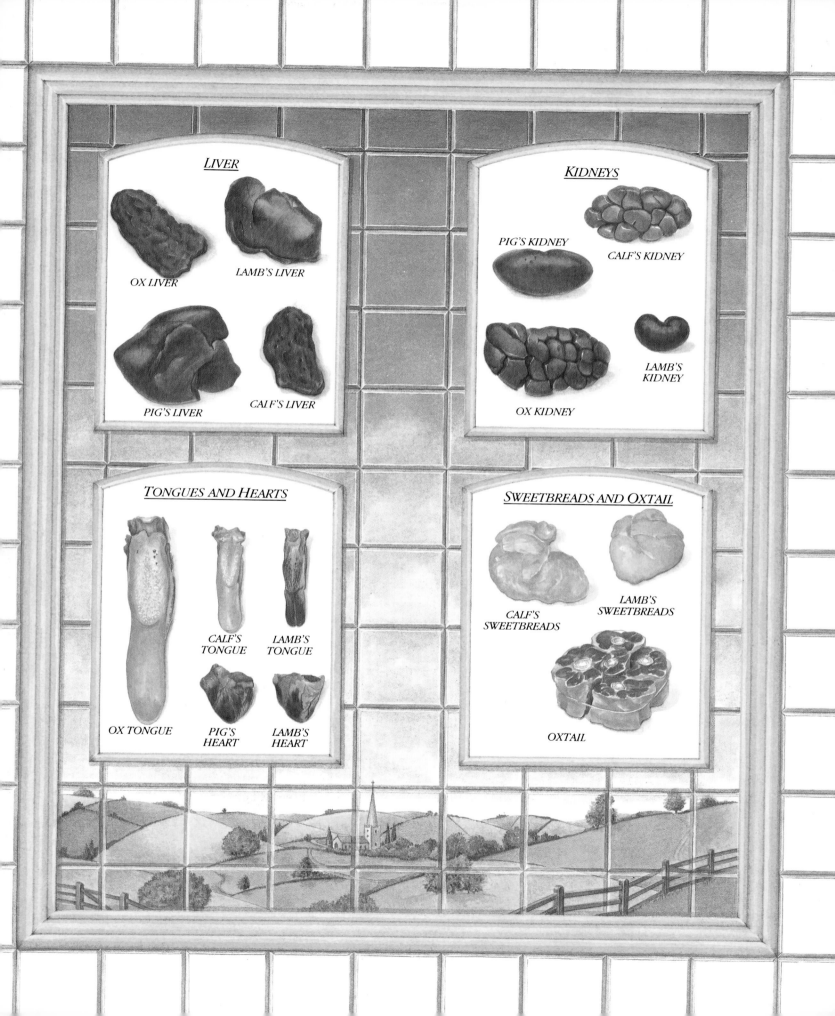

HOW TO COOK OFFAL

Offal is different from other types of meat in that each type is best cooked in a particular way. Roasting, for instance, is generally only used for hearts. Stewing, casseroling, frying and grilling are all often used for offal. The microwave is good for offal cooking, too.

Most offal, particularly liver and kidneys, has no fat of its own, so it is important when grilling or frying to ensure there is sufficient fat or other liquid to keep it succulent. Offal should not be overcooked, either, or it will dry out and become rather hard. Liver and kidneys may be cooked on a barbecue, but are best if marinated first.

Liver

All liver is excellent nutritional value but varies in texture and flavour. It should always look smooth and glossy. Wash and remove any loose pieces of skin and veins before cooking. Take care not to overcook or it may become tough and uninteresting.

CALF'S LIVER The superlative liver, also very much more expensive than the other types. Very tender and delicately flavoured, needing only very light cooking. Either grill or fry.

LAMB'S LIVER Cheaper than calves' and has the next best flavour. It is the most popular and versatile. Grill or fry when cut into slices; or cube to add to casseroles or

COOKING OFFAL IN THE MICROWAVE

This is not really the best way to cook most kinds of offal, although liver, when cut into strips, and kidneys, when skinned and cut into slices, cook quite well with the use of a browning dish.

In the chart below, the offal was tested in a 650–700 watt cooker. Always follow the instructions in your own microwave's handbook for cooking offal.

CUT	TIME FOR 450 g/1 lb	STANDING TIME	SPECIAL POINTS
Liver	5–6 mins		Use browning dish. Cut into strips. Cook on 100% power.
Kidney	6–8 mins		Use browning dish. Remove outer skin and slice. Cook on 100% power.

stews, or barbecue when wrapped in bacon.

PIG'S LIVER Coarser and very strongly flavoured. It can be soaked in milk for an hour prior to cooking to reduce the pungency. Grill, fry, braise or casserole. Probably the best to use for pâtés.

OX LIVER Fairly cheap but has a strong flavour and can be tough. Best to casserole or stew, usually cut into cubes; or use for pâté.

Kidneys

Ox and calf's kidneys are many-lobed, elongated, coarse and have a strong flavour. They are traditionally casseroled and

used in pies and casseroles either sliced, cubed, or cut into smaller pieces. Also used with stewing steak for steak and kidney pies and puddings.

Pig's and lamb's kidneys are 'kidney' shaped with pig's kidney having a much stronger and pungent flavour and being larger. They are often fried or grilled because they need to be cooked quickly to keep them tender. Pan frying is also a good method. Always wash kidneys very thoroughly and remove the skin and central core before cooking. Sometimes, lamb's kidneys can be bought still in the suet which surrounds them; in which case simply ease them out before preparing.

Preparing liver

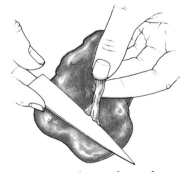

Cut away any tubes and membrane

Preparing kidneys

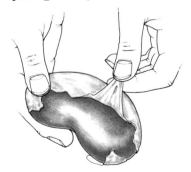

1 Peel off the fine membrane

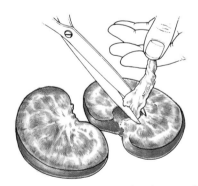

2 Halve the kidney and snip out the core

Tongue

This should not be thought of as something to be served cold – it is delicious hot or served in a casserole. Ox and lamb's tongues are the most commonly used and they can both be bought fresh or salted. The skin should be smooth, for the tongue becomes rough as it ages. It is best to soak a salted tongue overnight in cold water before cooking. Salted and smoked tongues require about half the cooking time of fresh tongues.

Ox tongue has the best flavour and texture and can be boiled or braised to serve hot or cold (sometimes set in its own jelly). Lamb's tongues are usually sold fresh and should be braised or casseroled. Once cooked, they should be skinned and then returned to the casserole before serving.

Oxtail

Oxtail is sold ready skinned and jointed and often tied together with string if bought from a butcher; or prepacked in varying sized amounts from a supermarket. One oxtail weighs about 1.5 kg/3 lb and it is excellent braised or stewed in a rich, tender and sustaining casserole or made into a delicious soup. It is a good idea to make an oxtail dish the day before it is required so it can be chilled and any fat removed before it is reheated for serving.

Heart

Four kinds are generally available: beef (ox), calf's, lamb's and pig's.

Heart is used for stews or casseroles and also for stuffing and roasting. It is an economical meat with very little waste or fat, has a marvellous flavour and is very full of nutrients. Wash all types of heart very thoroughly in several bowls of cold running water and remove all the tubes and arteries.

Ox heart is the largest, weighing up to 2.75 kg/6 lb, and to casserole it should be cut into strips or cubes. It can also be parboiled, stuffed (or not) and casseroled, braised or roasted. All these methods need to be slow, to tenderize the meat. Calf's

AVERAGE AMOUNTS OF OFFAL TO ALLOW	
TYPES OF MEAT	AMOUNTS PER PERSON
Liver	100 g/4 oz per portion.

Kidneys: ox
  calf's
  lamb's
  pig's
	100 g/4 oz per portion;
	1 will serve 1–2 portions;
	allow 2 per portion;
	1–2 per portion, depending on size.

Tongue: ox
 	
  calf's
  lamb's
	1 will serve 8 portions when hot, a little more when cold;
	1 will serve 3–4;
	1

Oxtail	1 will serve 3–4 portions.

Hearts: ox
  calf's
  lamb's
	1 will serve 4–6 portions;
	1 will serve 2 portions;
	1

Sweetbreads	100 g/4 oz or 1 pair per portion.
Brains	1–2 sets per portion.
Tripe	100–175 g/4–6 oz per portion.

hearts are smaller and more tender but still need slow cooking. Lamb's hearts are the most tender and popular and are usually stuffed and braised, roasted or pot roasted. Pig's hearts have a stronger flavour but can be prepared as for lamb's hearts.

Sweetbreads

Calf's are the more delicate of the sweetbreads sold, though lamb's are the more readily available. They should be soaked in cold water for 20 minutes and then simmered in water with lemon juice added for 20 minutes. Plunge into cold water then remove any tubes and outer membrane. When dry they can be stewed, braised or fried when they are often coated in egg and crumbs first.

Brains

These are used from lamb and calves. One set of lamb's brains will feed one portion whilst calf's will serve two. They have a delicate flavour and are usually sold in sets.

They must be bought, prepared, cooked and served whilst very fresh. Often a butcher will ask customers to order brains as they do not keep if unsold. They should be soaked in cold water for 15 minutes, before being put into a pan of cold water. Bring to the boil and simmer for 10 minutes, then proceed as for sweetbreads.

Tripe

This is the stomach lining of the ox. The smooth or 'blanket' tripe comes from the smooth first stomach and is sometimes also called 'plain'; from the second stomach comes 'honeycomb' tripe because that exactly describes it; tripe from the third stomach is called 'thick seam'. All should be thick, firm and white. It is usually sold 'dressed', which means it has been partly boiled. There is no difference in taste among the varieties, only in texture, and often you will buy packs which contain some of each kind. It is often served in a white sauce with onions; but is also good when coated in egg and crumbs and fried; or casseroled in various ways.

Miscellaneous

Pig's and sheep's heads are available, often halved before sale. The best brawn is made from a pig's head although it is now sometimes made from sheep's or occasionally a calf's. Pig's cheek is also sold to boil, coat in egg and breadcrumbs and then fry, when it is known as Bath Chaps and is particularly popular in the north of England. A whole pig's head can be boiled or roasted and glazed and decorated to serve as Boar's Head to grace a special cold buffet table.

Trotters

When cooked, pig's trotters or feet produce a protein-rich gelatine used to make jellied stock which is an essential part of meat pies and moulds. They have always been very popular in international cuisines, but not so popular in Britain. Pig's trotters are the most widely used and the meat from them too can be put into brawn. They can be parboiled and then roasted to make a very tasty dish. Calf's trotters are traditionally used for aspic.

STORING OFFAL

It is very important to cook offal when very fresh, preferably buying and cooking it on the same day. Otherwise, it must be stored, covered, in the refrigerator as soon as it is brought home and used the next day.

Freezing offal

If bought fresh (i.e. not previously frozen), offal can be wrapped and stored in the freezer for 2–3 months. First of all, make absolutely sure that it is fresh and not thawed from frozen.

With kidneys, wrap each one separately before putting into a large freezer polythene bag. Liver can be frozen in a piece or sliced; if sliced, it is best to separate each slice with freezer film. Oxtail will freeze ready cut up. Heads, trotters, tripe, brains and sweetbreads are better bought fresh from the butcher. They may be frozen after cooking for up to 2 months.

Cooked offal dishes which have been casseroled or braised can be frozen for up to 1 month, as can pâtés containing offal. However, fried or grilled offal should not be frozen because it dries out too much and loses texture and taste. Salted or pickled cooked offal (tongue etc.) should not be

frozen. When cooked offal is frozen it should be only for a short period and, although safe for the time suggested above, is better eaten as soon as possible.

If the offal has been bought ready-frozen it may be put into a freezer at home if it has just begun to thaw but is still very cold. If it has really thawed, it must be cooked first before re-freezing.

Always thaw out frozen offal completely before using it, and cook it as soon as possible after thawing.

BUYING OFFAL

When buying offal, always choose pieces which look fresh and moist, have a good colour and smell fresh.

Liver should have little, if any, smell. Kidneys should smell fresh and show a good colour. Sweetbreads should be pale in colour and look 'bright'. Brains, too, should be bright and fresh-looking, have a clean smell and a pinky-grey colour.

It may not always be possible to smell offal in a supermarket, where it will almost always have been carefully wrapped or packed in well-sealed plastic containers or bags, so you must be guided by appearance, colour and the date on the pack label.

NUTRIENT CONTENT OF OFFAL							
	ENERGY kcal	PROTEIN g	FAT g	PER 100g IRON mg	VITAMIN A μg	VITAMIN D μg	RIBOFLAVIN mg
Roast sheep heart	237	26.1	14.7	8.1	—	—	1.5
Stewed ox kidney	172	25.6	7.7	8.0	150	—	2.1
Raw lamb's liver	179	20.1	10.3	9.4	19,900	0.5	3.3
Fried lamb's liver	232	22.9	14.0	10.0	30,500	0.5	4.4
Stewed oxtail, meat only	243	30.5	13.4	3.8	20,100	1.1	3.6
Raw lamb's sweetbread	131	15.3	7.8	1.7	—	—	0.3
Boiled ox tongue	293	19.5	23.9	3.0	—	—	0.3
Stewed tripe	100	14.8	4.5	0.7	—	—	0.1

OXTAIL CASSEROLE

1 oxtail, cut up
2–3 tablespoons oil or dripping
25 g/1 oz plain flour
600 ml/1 pint beef stock or water
2 large onions, peeled and chopped
4 carrots, peeled and sliced
3–4 sticks celery, sliced
1 leek, trimmed and sliced (optional)
salt and black pepper
1 teaspoon paprika
1 teaspoon curry powder
1 teaspoon Worcestershire sauce
2 bay leaves
16 black olives
freshly chopped mixed herbs or parsley,
*   to garnish*

Trim any excess fat from the pieces of oxtail. Heat the oil or dripping in a large heavy-based saucepan and fry the pieces of oxtail until well browned all over. Remove from the pan. Pour off all but 1½ tablespoons fat from the pan.

Stir the flour into the fat and cook for 1 minute, then gradually add the stock or water and bring up to the boil.

Add the onions, carrots, celery, leek, plenty of seasonings, paprika, curry powder, Worcestershire sauce and bay leaves and replace the oxtail. Either cover the pan tightly and simmer very gently for about 3 hours on top of the stove or transfer the contents of the pan to a large ovenproof casserole and cook in a very moderate oven (160°C, 325°F, Gas Mark 3) for 3½–4 hours. The meat must be very tender before serving.

If possible, cool the casserole and chill overnight so the layer fat that forms on the surface can be easily removed. Discard the bay leaves and add the olives. If there is not time to cool and chill the casserole, spoon off as much excess fat from the surface as possible before serving.

If reheating, this must be done thoroughly either in a saucepan by bringing to the boil and simmering gently for about 20 minutes, or in the same temperature oven for about an hour. Sprinkle with chopped herbs and serve.

SERVES 3–4

NOTE: half the stock or water can be replaced with red or white wine, if preferred.

from MARGARET THATCHER MP
LAMB CHOPS IN A PARCEL

The Prime Minister, the Rt. Hon. MARGARET THATCHER, was pleased to have the opportunity to promote the home market, and sent from Downing Street this recipe for lamb chops; it is one she particularly enjoys.

8 lamb chops

Home-made stuffing
75 g/3 oz fresh breadcrumbs (preferably brown)
mixed herbs to taste
salt and black pepper
dash of nutmeg
2 medium onions, peeled and finely chopped
1 egg, beaten
hot water, to mix

225 g/8 oz peas
2 medium onions, peeled and chopped
1 teaspoon sugar

Preheat the oven to moderate (180°C, 350°F, Gas Mark 4). Trim the chops, if necessary.

To make the stuffing, mix all the stuffing ingredients together in a bowl, using just enough hot water to make the mixture soft, but not soggy.

Grease the centre of four 30 cm/12 inch squares of kitchen foil with left-over fat or cooking oil, and spread up to 1 cm/½ inch thick with the home-made stuffing.

Place two lamb chops on each piece of foil, and roll up into a parcel, securing all the edges by rolling them over.

Bake the parcels in a preheated moderate oven for up to 30 minutes, depending on how well-cooked you like your chops.

Meanwhile, prepare the peas cooked with onions. Sauté the onions until soft in a little fat or oil. Drain well. Put the peas in a pan with salt, the drained onions and a heaped teaspoonful of sugar. Add a teacup of boiling water, and bring to the boil. Simmer for 5–8 minutes, then drain.

Serve the lamb parcels with the peas cooked with onions.

SERVES 4

from MICHAEL MACKENZIE
CALF'S LIVER WITH BASIL SAUCE

The basil in this favourite recipe of MICHAEL MACKENZIE, Director-General of the *Food and Drink Federation*, comes from the Pesto sauce, a classic Italian sauce composed of basil, olive oil, pine kernels and Parmesan cheese. The sauce is now widely available in supermarkets in Britain.

25 g/1 oz butter
1 tablespoon oil
4 slices calf's liver, thinly sliced
2 teaspoons Pesto sauce
150 ml/¼ pint double cream or Greek yogurt, or a mixture of the two
salt and black pepper
a little stock (optional)
chopped parsley, to garnish

Heat the butter and oil in a large frying pan until it is very hot. Carefully add the liver and fry for 2–3 minutes on each side. Remove from the pan to a serving dish and keep hot.

Add the Pesto sauce, cream and/or yogurt and salt and pepper to the pan and stir well to mix. Add a little stock if the sauce seems too thick. Bring to the boil, stirring all the time, then pour over the liver. Sprinkle with the chopped parsley and serve at once.

SERVES 4

RIGHT Lamb chops in a parcel

from NEIL KINNOCK MP
WELSH LAMB

The Rt. Hon. NEIL KINNOCK, *Leader of the Labour Party*, gives this book the flavour of traditional Welsh cookery with these recipes for leg of lamb and its accompanying vegetable 'cake'.

large leg of Welsh lamb
salt and black pepper
1 teaspoon ground ginger
1 tablespoon honey
2 tablespoons rosemary
bottle of dry cider

Preheat the oven to moderate (160°C, 325°F, Gas Mark 3).

Rub the lamb with the salt, pepper and ginger and spread the honey over it. Put it into a pan or casserole with a lid and scatter the rosemary over the meat. Pour in the cider to about 5cm/2 inches up the pan. Place the covered casserole in the preheated oven and cook for about 1½ hours, depending on how pink you like lamb. Baste the meat regularly during cooking.

Strain the juice into a saucepan and boil rapidly to reduce it to make a beautiful sauce.

Serve the lamb with Feiser Nionod (Onion Cake). See recipe below.

FEISER NIONOD *(Onion Cake)*

1 kg/2 lb firm potatoes
450 g/1 lb onions, peeled and chopped
100 g/4 oz butter
salt and black pepper

Preheat the oven to moderately hot (200°C, 400°F, Gas Mark 6).

Peel or scrape the potatoes and cut into paper-thin slices (I do this with a food processor). Wash the slices well in plenty of cold water to remove starch, and dry. You can arrange the cake in a buttered tin and turn it out for serving, or use a shallow casserole or gratin dish. Arrange alternate layers of potatoes and onions dotted with butter and well seasoned. If the potato is above the top of the dish, don't worry as it will cook down. Cover with foil.

Bake for 1 hour in the preheated oven. For the last 15 minutes, remove the foil.

SERVES 8

from ROY ACKERMAN
LOIN OF PORK WITH PEASE PUDDING

ROY ACKERMAN, chef, restaurateur, one-time Deputy Chairman of Kennedy Brooks, and publisher, also became a television personality in 1989, originating and presenting the series *The Chef's Apprentice*, a history of food. This fine modern adaptation of a medieval recipe which is also a good example of British regional cooking, was written for the book of the television series.

900 g/2 lb loin of pork (boned, rolled and salted)
2 medium carrots
2 medium onions
1 leek
2 celery stalks
3–4 parsley stalks
½ bay leaf
1 sprig thyme
6 peppercorns
450 g/1 lb yellow split peas
50 g/2 oz butter
2 egg yolks

Ask the butcher to prepare the pork and to salt it for you. Soak overnight in cold water before cooking.

Put the pork into a saucepan and cover with cold water. Bring to the boil and remove any scum that rises to the surface. Reduce the heat and simmer gently for 10 minutes.

Add one carrot, one onion, the leek, celery, herbs and peppercorns and continue to simmer for a further hour.

Meanwhile, put the split peas into a separate saucepan with the remaining onion and carrot and cover with cold water. Bring to the boil, and remove any scum that rises to the surface. Add salt and simmer for about an hour, until tender.

When the peas are soft, remove the carrot and onion and drain the peas. Purée the peas, adding butter and pepper.

To mould the purée, beat in the egg yolks, then pour the mixture into individual moulds. Stand these in a pan and pour hot water into the pan to come about half way up the sides of the moulds.

Put the pan into an oven preheated to moderate (180°C, 350°F, Gas Mark 4) and bake until firm, about 40 minutes.

To serve, remove the pork from its cooking liquor, carve into slices and serve with a little of the cooking liquor.

Unmould the puddings and serve at the side of the pork slices. (If not moulded, serve the pease pudding separately in a vegetable dish.)

Plain vegetables such as carrots, turnips, beans or cabbage can be served as an accompaniment to this dish.

SERVES 4–6

NOTE: to avoid wasting the vegetables – and this also enables you to prepare 2 dishes at the same time – cook an additional 100 g/4 oz split peas with the peas for this dish. Then purée this extra amount with the carrot, onion and cooking liquor (none of which is needed for this dish) in a blender to give you a delicious soup.

LEFT Welsh lamb with feiser nionod

from GEOFFREY JOHN
CIG MOCH CHABETS
(*Boiled ham with parsley sauce*)

This traditional Welsh recipe for boiled ham comes from GEOFFREY JOHN, Chairman of the *Meat and Livestock Commission*. He remembers it as a favourite from his childhood in South Wales.

1.25–1.5 kg/2½–3 lb forehock or collar bacon
1 large onion, peeled and stuck with cloves
½ lemon
1 teaspoon brown sugar
300 ml/½ pint cider
450 g/1 lb white cabbage, chopped
1 kg/2 lb potatoes, peeled
300 ml/½ pint Parsley sauce (see recipe below)

Soak the bacon in cold water overnight.

Next day, drain the bacon and put into a large pan with the onion, lemon, sugar and cider. Add cold water to just cover the joint. Bring to the boil and simmer for 20 minutes per 450 g/1 lb.

Remove the joint from the pan, take off the skin and discard and keep the joint in a warm place.

Put the cabbage into the bacon liquid and cook until just tender. Drain, reserving the cooking liquid, and keep warm. Boil the potatoes in a separate pan of water.

To serve, slice the joint and place on a warmed serving plate with the vegetables.

Make the Parsley sauce (see below), using 300 ml/½ pint of the cooking liquid, and pour over the cabbage and potatoes.
SERVES 6

PARSLEY SAUCE
25 g/1 oz butter
25 g/1 oz plain flour
300 ml/½ pint milk, stock or cooking liquid
salt and black pepper
50 g/2 oz chopped parsley

Melt the butter in a pan, stir in the flour and cook, stirring, for one minute. Remove from the heat and gradually beat in the liquid and salt and pepper to taste. Return to the heat, bring to the boil and cook for 2 minutes, stirring constantly.

When the sauce is cooked, stir in the parsley.

from DEREK COOPER
JANET COOPER'S LEFTOVER MUTTON PIE

The BBC's 'food and drink' man, DEREK COOPER, makes a nostalgic trip back in time to childhood meals for this recipe.

'As we live for a part of the year in the Isle of Skye, where sheep outnumber humans by 15 to one, it's not perhaps surprising that, when we tire of fish, we eat quite a lot of lamb and mutton. My earliest memories of mutton are of Sabbath lunches which almost inevitably began with Scotch broth made from the goodness of barley and a couple of pounds of mutton. We ate the soup first and then attacked the joint. The meat had been, not unnaturally, very well boiled and in the broth we'd probably had the best of it. When Dr Johnson first encountered Scotch broth on his tour to the Hebrides he relished it. Boswell watched him eat several platefuls in Aberdeen and said, "You never eat it before, sir." "No, sir," replied Johnson, "but I don't care how soon I eat it again."

'What Meg Dods called "the bland, balsamic barley-broth of Scotland" is best made with neck or shoulder of mutton; the meat from a three-year-old sheep is arguably the best. When we have any mutton left over from a roast we make a mutton pie. When I say "we" make it I mean my wife Janet makes it while I hang around the kitchen getting in the way.

'This is what she does. She first of all makes a shortcrust pastry with 350 g/12 oz of flour and 175 g/6 oz of butter and lard plus a round tablespoonful of icing sugar.

'Make the pastry in the usual way. Take 450 g/1 lb of cold cooked mutton (or lamb) and 350 g/12 oz of sausage meat, a pinch of thyme and a generous glass of cognac. Cut the meat into thin slices. Gather up any scraps and chop finely and then mix them into the sausage meat. Add a finely chopped clove of garlic.

'Butter a loose-bottomed cake tin about 20 cm/8 inch in diameter and 5cm/2 inch deep and line it with the rolled-out pastry, having laid aside enough to form a lid. Arrange half the sausage meat on the bottom of the pie. Sprinkle with a little thyme. Add a layer of meat, sprinkle with salt and pepper and dowse with cognac. Repeat once.

'Roll out the remaining pastry, lay over the pie to form a lid, crimp the border and make a hole in the centre. Brush with egg yolk and cook for ten minutes in a hot oven (220°C, 425°F, Gas Mark 7) then lower to moderate (180°C, 350°F, Gas Mark 4) and cook for about 40 minutes. At the last moment pour a little melted butter or gravy into the hole. The pie is equally delicious served hot or cold. If you serve it hot none will be left over to eat cold, especially if anybody with an appetite like Dr Johnson's is around.'

RIGHT Janet Cooper's leftover mutton pie

from WALTER GOLDSMITH
LAMB STEW WITH LENTILS AND HARICOT BEANS

This recipe from WALTER GOLDSMITH, Chairman of *Food from Britain*, passes his 'mouth-water test' with flying colours. 'These are dishes which get top marks, since the mere thought of the flavour of them will excite my taste buds!' he explains.

15 g/$\frac{1}{2}$ oz butter
450 g/1 lb lean boneless lamb (leg or shoulder) cut into 2.5 cm/1 inch cubes
1.2 l/2 pints stock
350 g/12 oz swede, diced
450 g/1 lb leeks, trimmed, sliced
100 g/4 oz haricot beans, soaked overnight, cooked for 30 minutes and drained
100 g/4 oz split red lentils
bouquet garni
salt and black pepper

Lamb stew with lentils and haricot beans

Melt the butter in a flameproof casserole on a high heat. Put in the lamb and brown it on all sides. Pour in the stock and bring to the boil. Add the swede, leeks, beans, lentils, bouquet garni, salt and pepper. Bring casserole back up to the boil.

Cover and simmer gently for 1$\frac{1}{4}$ hours, or until the lamb is tender.

SERVES 4

from SALLY PROCTOR
BOEUF PHILIPPE

This is one of the recipes cooked at *Leith's School of Food & Wine*, and comes from the Principal, SALLY PROCTOR.

500 g/1¼ lb fillet of beef (ends will do)
Worcestershire sauce
black pepper
1 tablespoon beef dripping
½ cauliflower, washed and cut into florets
175 g/6 oz French beans, topped and tailed
3 tomatoes
½ teaspoon horseradish sauce
1 garlic clove, peeled and crushed
3 tablespoons French dressing
8 black olives, stoned
bunch of watercress

Preheat the oven to moderately hot (200°C, 400°F, Gas Mark 6).

Season the meat with Worcestershire sauce and black pepper. Heat the beef dripping in a roasting tin over the cooker ring and add the beef. Brown evenly on all sides. If the beef is in one thick piece put it into the oven for 15 minutes – less if it is thin or in smaller pieces. It should be just pink inside. Allow to cool.

Plunge the cauliflower florets into a pan of boiling water for 4–5 minutes. Drain and rinse under cold water to prevent further cooking. Drain again.

Cook the prepared beans in boiling salted water for 5 minutes and then rinse under cold water and drain.

Plunge the tomatoes into boiling water for 5 seconds and then peel. Cut into quarters.

Add the horseradish sauce and the garlic to the French dressing. The salad is now ready for assembly but this should not be done until just before serving. The beef will lose its colour if dressed up too soon, and the salad will look tired if left to stand for any length of time.

Cut the beef into thin slices and then into thin strips, cutting *across* the grain of the

Boeuf Philippe

meat. Place in a basin with the other ingredients, reserving one tomato and 4 olives for decoration.

Using your hands, mix in three-quarters of the French dressing and pile into a serving dish. Place the reserved olives and tomatoes on top of the dish and brush with a little French dressing. Garnish with a bunch of watercress dipped in the remaining dressing.

SERVES 6

NATIONAL
WOMEN'S MAGAZINES

from GILL MACLENNAN
PORK AND BAMBOO CURRY

Spices add a touch of the Orient to this pork recipe from GILL MACLENNAN, Cookery Editor of *Woman*.

500 g/1 lb 4 oz lean pork
198 g/7 oz can bamboo shoots
2 tablespoons oil
1 large onion, peeled and chopped
2.5 cm/1 inch fresh root ginger, chopped
4 garlic cloves, peeled and crushed
1 tablespoon turmeric
1½ teaspoons mild curry powder
1 × 397 g/14 oz can tomatoes
300 ml/½ pint chicken stock (made with a cube)
salt and black pepper

Cut the pork into 1.5 cm/½ inch cubes. Drain the bamboo shoots and cut into sticks.

Heat the oil in a large pan, add the onion, ginger and garlic and fry for 10 minutes, until golden. Add the pork, turmeric and curry powder and stir to seal the meat. Add the bamboo shoots, tomatoes, stock, salt and pepper. Stir well.

Bring to the boil, cover and simmer gently for 1 hour, until oil rises to surface. Serve with rice or noodles.

SERVES 4

from ALEX BARKER
BARBECUED SHOULDER OF LAMB IN RED WINE

'This is a favourite barbecue summertime recipe of ours', says ALEX BARKER, Cookery Editor of *Prima*, who provided this recipe. 'It makes full use of the barbecue, yet you have a roast, or at least something to carve!

'This recipe can be done with a leg of lamb, where the meat is denser and leaner. However, I think the slightly fattier shoulder cut suits the rigours of barbecue cooking much better, having its own basting to prevent drying out. It can be cooked in a good size grill – very useful to resort to if your barbecue is not under cover! If you choose a shoulder, it should be boned so that it can be opened out almost flat, in one long piece. Cut into the joint slightly so there isn't too much of a bump in the middle.'

1 shoulder of lamb, approx. boned weight 1½ kg/3 lb

Marinade
2–3 garlic cloves, peeled and crushed
150 ml/¼ pint red wine
300 ml/½ pint oil
2 tablespoons clear honey
salt and black pepper
2 sprigs rosemary

Lay out the boned shoulder of lamb in a large tin or dish, so it is as flat as possible. Rub the crushed garlic all over. Then mix the remaining ingredients together and pour over the lamb. Leave, covered, in the refrigerator for at least 1–2 hours, or overnight.

When you are ready to cook the meat and the barbecue is really hot, remove the lamb from the marinade, reserving it for basting with. Brush the barbecue rack with oil and place the sprigs of herbs on top, then the lamb, skin side downwards. Baste the top with oil and then turn over after 10 minutes. Repeat this once more each side, by which time the lamb should be sufficiently cooked. Or continue as long as you wish, for well done meat. Baste with more marinade just before carving.

Serve the lamb with salads and brown rice with toasted nuts.

SERVES 6–8

RIGHT Barbecued shoulder of lamb in red wine

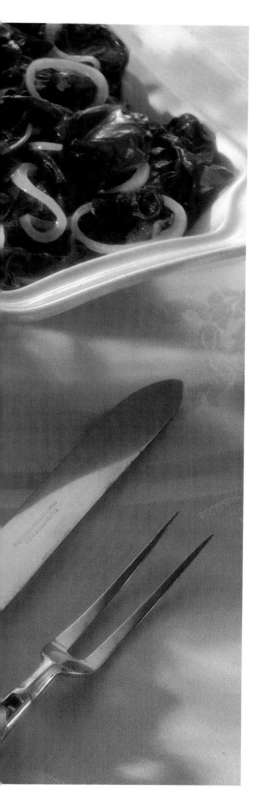

from SARA LEWIS
CROWN ROAST OF PORK

This recipe was created for *Family Circle* magazine and cookery editor SARA LEWIS reports some very positive reactions from her readers. They thought it was meatier than a crown roast of lamb, and they raved about the stuffing!

1 prepared, but not stuffed, crown roast of
* pork*
1 onion, peeled
225 g/8 oz carrots
225 g/8 oz parsnips
1 teaspoon cumin seeds
1 teaspoon coriander seeds
2 tablespoons oil
½ teaspoon turmeric
225 g/8 oz coarse pork sausage meat
50 g/2 oz fresh breadcrumbs
pork skin for crackling

Preheat the oven to hot (220°C, 425°F, Gas Mark 7).

Finely chop the onion. Peel and coarsely grate the carrots and parsnips. Crush the cumin and coriander seeds in a pestle and mortar or using a rolling pin in a basin.

Heat half the oil in a frying pan, add the onion and cook for 3 minutes until softened. Add two-thirds of the grated carrot and parsnip, crushed seeds and turmeric and cook for 1 minute. Reserve the remaining carrot and parsnip.

Break up the sausage meat in a large bowl, stir in the vegetable mixture and breadcrumbs and add seasoning to taste.

Place the crown of pork on a large piece of foil and press the stuffing into the centre to give a good round shape. Weigh and calculate the cooking time, allowing 10 minutes at high temperature, then 30 minutes per 450 g/1 lb.

Place the crown of pork (still on the foil) in a roasting pan. Cover the rib ends with foil and cook in the preheated oven, reducing the temperature after 10 minutes to moderate (180°C, 350°F, Gas Mark 4).

Score the pork skin and rub in a little salt. Place on a small baking sheet and cook on the shelf above the pork for the last 40 minutes of cooking time.

Transfer the crown roast to a warmed serving plate. Remove the foil from the rib tips. Cover the pan with foil and leave to rest for 10 minutes. Meanwhile, make gravy in the usual way. Fry the reserved grated carrot and parsnip in oil for 2 minutes. Spoon over the centre of the crown roast and top with the pork crackling, cut into strips. Remove the string. Garnish the plate with a few sprigs of watercress or carrot tops. Serve with gravy, roast potatoes and stir-fried spinach.

SERVES 6

from MANDY NORWOOD
PORK GRANVILLE

MANDY NORWOOD, Deputy Editor of *MORE*, appreciates this recipe for its easy preparation and good flavour.

450 g/1 lb pork fillet
1 green pepper, seeded and cubed
1 red pepper, seeded and cubed
1 medium-sized onion, peeled and diced
black pepper
4 tomatoes, sliced
10 mushrooms, sliced
tomato ketchup, to taste
120 ml/4 fl oz water

Slice the pork into medium-sized pieces and put with all the other ingredients into a casserole. Leave to marinate overnight.

Next day, preheat the oven to moderate (180°C, 350°F, Gas Mark 4). Add extra water to the casserole to fill it up to about one-third, place in the preheated oven and cook for about 1 hour.

SERVES 4

LEFT Crown roast of pork

from CAROLINE RICHMOND WALKER
LOINS OF LAMB WITH OATMEAL

This is a favourite recipe of CAROLINE RICHMOND WALKER, Cookery Editor of *Good Housekeeping*, because it is simple to prepare and serve, while the thyme and soft cheese complement the sweetness of the lamb beautifully. Caroline's tips for the preparation of Loins of Lamb with Oatmeal are:

Trim away as much excess fat as possible before stuffing and coating the joints of lamb.

Use fine string for tying the joints or the coating will be pulled away when the string is removed.

Stuff and coat the joints in the morning ready to cook later; they can also be frozen at this stage provided that fresh, not previously frozen lamb, has been used.

It's easy to bone the lamb yourself but, given prior warning, most butchers will do it for you.

2 × 1.1 kg/2½ lb loins of lamb
150 g/5 oz low-fat soft cheese
2 tablespoons fresh chopped thyme (or 1
  teaspoon dried)
2 garlic cloves, peeled and crushed
salt and black pepper
plain flour
1 egg
100 g/4 oz medium oatmeal
polyunsaturated oil
600 ml/1 pint stock
sherry
fresh thyme or garnish (optional)

Preheat the oven to moderately hot (200°C, 400°F, Gas Mark 6).

Using a sharp knife, cut all bones away from the lamb and trim off excess fat.

Beat together the cheese, herbs, crushed garlic and seasonings. Spread half over the fleshy side of each boned loin. Roll up the lamb to enclose the stuffing completely. Tie with fine string.

Roll the joints in a little flour then brush with beaten egg and coat with the oatmeal, pressing firmly to ensure that the oatmeal clings to the joint.

Heat a thin coating of oil in a medium-sized roasting tin. Add the joints. Roast in the preheated oven for 45–50 minutes. Baste once during cooking.

Remove the joints from the oven and thickly slice them, discarding the string; cover and keep warm in a low oven.

Pour off any excess fat from the roasting tin, leaving about 2 tablespoons. Stir in 4 teaspoons flour and cook, stirring, until browned. Add the stock and bring to the boil, stirring. Cook for 1–2 minutes. Add a dash of sherry. Adjust seasoning and serve with the lamb. Garnish with fresh thyme.

SERVES 6

from GINA STEER
LAMB WITH ALMONDS

This recipe is a particular favourite of GINA STEER, Cookery Editor of *Woman's Own*, and is ideal for entertaining. Gina loves the orangey mint flavour with lamb. The almonds give the dish a good 'crunch'. A good hint from Gina: when preparing cubes of lamb, buy either lamb fillet or top end of leg and remember to cut with the grain of the meat.

750 g–1 kg/1½–2 lb lean lamb, preferably
  from the leg or fillet
salt and black pepper
2 tablespoons plain flour
2 tablespoons butter or margarine
100 g/4 oz slivered blanched almonds
450 ml/¾ pint lamb or chicken stock
4 tablespoons Grand Marnier
finely grated rind and juice of 1 orange
1 teaspoon mint sauce concentrate
2 oranges, peeled and segmented
mint sprigs, to garnish

Trim and discard any fat from the lamb and cut the meat into 2.5 cm/1 inch cubes. Season, then coat in the flour, reserving any excess flour.

Heat the fat in a pan. Add the almonds and cook over a moderate heat until golden brown. Remove, drain on absorbent kitchen paper and set aside.

Add the meat to the pan and brown all over. Sprinkle in the reserved flour and cook for a further 2 minutes. Stir in the stock, Grand Marnier, orange rind and juice and the mint sauce concentrate. Bring to the boil, then cover and simmer for 35–45 minutes, or until the meat is tender. Add the reserved almonds and half the orange segments. Continue to cook for a further 10 minutes. Adjust seasoning, if necessary.

Serve the lamb garnished with the remaining orange segments and mint sprigs.

SERVES 4

RIGHT Lamb with almonds

from MARIE-PIERRE MOINE
PORK CHOPS WITH ONION

'A very simple comforting supper dish,' says MARIE-PIERRE MOINE, Editor of *Taste*, of this beautifully flavoured recipe. 'The cider vinegar and honey gives the sauce a nice lift.'

4 pork chops, not too lean
large garlic clove, cut in half
1 teaspoon dried thyme
1 teaspoon dried sage
freshly ground black pepper
a little groundnut oil
a little butter
1 large onion, peeled and thinly sliced into
  rings
300 ml/½ pint dry cider
1 tablespoon cider vinegar
1 tablespoon honey
4 tablespoons single cream
salt (optional)
4 fresh sage leaves, to garnish

Rub the chops well with the cut side of the garlic, the dried herbs and plenty of pepper. Cover and leave at room temperature for an hour or so.

About 45 minutes before serving, heat a little oil and butter in a heavy-based pan large enough to take the 4 chops in a single layer. Slash the fat around the chops at 2.5 cm/1 inch intervals and put them in the pan.

Brown the chops well in the hot fat on both sides then remove and reserve.

Add a little more oil and butter to the pan if necessary, and soften the onion rings in it. Remove and reserve.

Pour the cider into the pan, scrape the bottom well and bring to a simmer. Add the chops, then the onion. Cover and cook gently for about 30 minutes, depending on thickness.

When the chops are cooked, remove them from the pan and keep warm. Reduce the juices a little if necessary then stir in the cider vinegar, honey and cream. Taste and adjust the seasoning. Spoon over the chops,

sprinkle with a little pepper and garnish each with a fresh sage leaf. Serve with mashed potatoes and spiced braised cabbage.

SERVES 4

from LIZ BURN
BEEF WITH GREEN PEAS

LIZ BURN, Cookery Editor of *Woman's Weekly*, traced this simple yet most delicious of recipes back to the 1940s. She says it can be cooked on top of the stove or even on a camping stove. It makes a good hot Sunday lunch dish, with any leftovers being sliced cold and served with a salad.

1 × 1–1.5 kg/2–3 lb piece silverside or
  topside
1 tablespoon oil
50 g/2 oz butter
salt and pepper
750 g–1 kg/1½–2 lb shelled fresh peas
  (for preference) or frozen
½ teaspoon sugar

In a frying pan, fry the meat in the oil and 25 g/1 oz of the butter until brown all over. Transfer it to a saucepan which just takes it comfortably and season with salt and pepper.

Fill all the space around the beef and the top with peas. Sprinkle with the sugar. Pour over any fat from the frying pan and dot over the remaining butter.

Cover the pan and cook, i.e. pot roast, the meat very gently for 1½–2 hours, depending on the size, until cooked.

SERVES 4–6

RIGHT Beef with green peas

from MITZIE WILSON
NEWTON POPPLEFORD PORK CASSEROLE

Other than straight roast pork with a good stuffing, MITZIE WILSON, Cookery Editor of *Best*, loves the classic Devon combination of cider, apples and pork, plus crème fraîche which gives this dish an irresistible creamy tart sauce. For want of an original name, she has called this recipe after her home village in Devon.

Newton Poppleford pork casserole

1 tablespoon vegetable oil
4 pork steaks or chops
225 g/8 oz gammon steak, cut into 2.5 cm/ 1 inch cubes
12 baby onions, peeled
100 g/4 oz button mushrooms, trimmed
2 tablespoons fresh tarragon
salt and black pepper
300 ml/½ pint dry cider
1 red-skinned apple, cored and thickly sliced
300 ml/½ pint crème fraîche
1 tablespoon cornflour
2 tablespoons water

Heat the oil and quickly fry the pork for three minutes, lightly browning it all over.

Add the gammon and cook for a further 2–3 minutes. Add the onions and fry for 2–3 minutes, then add the mushrooms, tarragon (reserving some for garnish), salt and pepper. Add just enough cider to cover.

Cover and cook over a low heat for 25 minutes, until the meat is tender. Add the apple and cook for 2–3 minutes. Stir in the crème fraîche.

Mix the cornflour and water together smoothly and stir in. Increase the heat and stir constantly until the sauce is thickened and no longer cloudy.

Serve the casserole garnished with tarragon.

SERVES 4

from RICHARD EHRLICH
JAPANESE-STYLE BEEF ROLLS

RICHARD EHRLICH, Food Editor of *Cosmopolitan* magazine, remembers, 'I had a dish like this years ago in a Japanese restaurant in New York City, and have wanted to reproduce it ever since. This is what I've come up with. The dish takes a few minutes to prepare and can serve as a starter or a main course.'

Japanese-style beef rolls

4 thick or 8 thin spring onions
4 tablespoons Kikkoman soy sauce
2 tablespoons sake
1 × 450 g/1 lb piece of well-trimmed Scottish beef fillet, cut from the thick end of the fillet
black pepper
corn oil

Cut off most of the green part of the spring onions and quarter or halve them lengthwise. Marinate them in the soy sauce and *sake* for 20 minutes.

Slice the beef into 16 pieces of approximately uniform thickness. (This is easier if the beef is well chilled or partially frozen).

Press the slices with your fingertips to flatten them out, and season with pepper. Roll each slice tightly around a spring onion, as if you were rolling a cigarette. If the spring onions protrude beyond the ends of the meat, trim off excess.

Preheat the grill at its highest heat. When it is very hot, brush the grill rack with corn oil and the beef rolls with marinade. Grill the rolls for 2–4 minutes, turning once. Do not overcook. Brush again with the marinade before turning and before serving.

Serve with *sake* or Japanese beer.

SERVES 2–4 AS A MAIN COURSE,
4–8 AS A STARTER

from TIM COTTERELL
HONEY AND MUSTARD ROAST PORK WITH APRICOT STUFFING

The *Daily Telegraph*'s Food and Drink Correspondent, TIM COTTERELL, likes this piquant version of roast pork.

1 × 4 kg/9 lb leg pork, with rind removed
  and reserved
1 garlic clove, peeled and crushed
3 tablespoons Dijon mustard
3 tablespoons clear honey
2 tablespoons oil
pinch marjoram
pinch dried sage
$\frac{1}{4}$ teaspoon ground ginger
salt and black pepper

Apricot stuffing
175 g/6 oz dried apricots, chopped
100 g/4 oz celery, finely chopped
175 g/6 oz fresh white breadcrumbs
$\frac{1}{2}$ teaspoon dried sage
$\frac{1}{4}$ teaspoon mixed spice
25 g/1 oz melted butter
salt and black pepper
1 egg
1 teaspoon Dijon mustard
lard, for cooking
2 teaspoons cornflour, mixed with
  a little water

Place the joint in a large roasting tin lined with foil. Combine the garlic, mustard, honey, oil, herbs and ginger. Season with salt and pepper and spread all over the joint. Cover lightly and leave overnight.

Next day, preheat the oven to moderate (160°C, 325°F, Gas Mark 3).

Wrap the foil over the joint and roast for 30 minutes per lb, plus 30 minutes, removing the foil for the last 35 minutes. Baste the joint and allow to brown.

Meanwhile, cut the pork rind into strips. Place in a tin, brush with oil and sprinkle with salt. Cook in the oven for about 1 hour until crisp.

For the apricot stuffing, mix all the stuffing ingredients together and shape into 12 balls. Place in a small roasting tin with a little lard and cook in the oven with the roast joint for the final 30–35 minutes' cooking time.

Remove the cooked joint from the roasting tin and allow to rest in a warm place for 10–15 minutes prior to carving. Drain off the remaining glaze and meat juices and thicken with the cornflour. Serve as a sauce with the meat.

SERVES 12–15

from SHEILA HUTCHINS
HAM IN CHABLIS

'Simple but sophisticated' is a good description of this delicious recipe from SHEILA HUTCHINS, Cookery Editor of the *Daily Express*.

2 shallots, peeled and evenly chopped
butter, for frying
100 g/4 oz button mushrooms, sliced
chopped parsley, to taste
1 garlic clove, peeled and chopped
4 thick slices cooked ham
wine glass of white wine (preferably
  Chablis)
1 tablespoon double cream

Brown the shallots in butter in a frying pan. Add the mushrooms, parsley and garlic. Put the cooked ham slices on top and pour a glass of white wine, preferably Chablis, over them. Let it simmer with a lid on for five minutes on a gentle heat.

Remove the ham to a hot dish with a slotted spoon.

Let the contents of the pan reduce over heat for a few minutes, then add a large tablespoon of thick cream. Heat the sauce, stirring, for a moment then pour it over the ham. Serve the dish piping hot.

SERVES 4

RIGHT Ham in chablis

from PRUE LEITH
BASIC MINCE

'Mince should be one of the great glories of cooking,' says PRUE LEITH, Food and Drink Correspondent for *The Guardian*. 'Savoury, syrupy and powerfully flavoured, good basic mince is the foundation of many a justly famous dish. Lasagne, Bolognese sauce for pasta, Moussaka, Chilli-con-carne, and Shepherd's Pie are all wonderful food.

'I swear the secret – the only secret – of good mince is in the frying.

'Few domestic cooks are prepared to fry fast enough to bespatter work surfaces and cooker – and impart the rich brown taste to the meat. Slowly-fried meat just stews greyly, losing its juices to the pan without browning at all.'

Here is Prue Leith's way to cook perfect mince.

750 g/1½ lb minced lean beef or lamb
100 g/4 oz chopped onion
oil for frying
1 tablespoon tomato purée
1 large garlic clove, peeled and crushed
300 ml/½ pint good strong stock
salt and black pepper

Use a heavy frying pan, not a saucepan. It is easier to see what's going on, and the open shape allows steam to escape. Heat the oil until *really* hot. Put a thin (1 cm/½ inch) layer of mince into the pan, flat like a huge burger. Press it down briefly, then *leave it alone* on full heat. The kitchen should smell like a barbecue. *Do not stir*. If you do, the meat won't get a chance to brown, and the juices will get a chance to escape, and you will be sweating/stewing rather than 'frying'.

After about three or four minutes at top heat turn the pancake of meat over, and fry the other side. If it breaks up, fine – just make sure all the bits get browned on the second side. Only when both sides of the meat are a good brown, stir and chop the

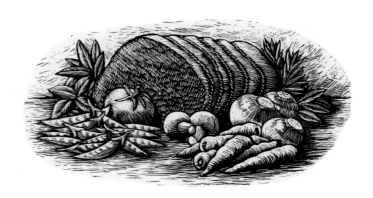

meat with a fish slice to separate the grains of mince. You don't want great big lumps, so keep at it until all pieces are evenly tiny. This 'chopping' of the mince is laborious but important.

Now tip the meat into a saucepan or casserole, and 'deglaze' the frying pan. This is really rinsing all the brown stuck bits off the bottom. Those dried-on juices contain a lot of flavour and you don't want to waste them. Pour a cup of water or stock (or wine, if you like) into the hot pan and stir and scrape while the liquid bubbles. Then pour on to the meat. If you still have more meat to fry, repeat the whole process, religiously.

Now you can flavour the basic mince as you will – with fried onions, shallots, mushrooms, with tomato purée, herbs, garlic. Then you need to add enough stock to make the whole pot liquid, and finally you must simmer it gently until the grains of meat are tender. Do this for at least an hour, stirring every so often to prevent the meat sticking and burning on the pan bottom. When done, the meat should be tender and the consistency thick and syrupy.

If the meat was properly trimmed and lean in the first place, little or no fat should escape during stewing to lie like an oil-slick on the surface. If it does, it needs removing, first by skimming, then by laying successive sheets of absorbent kitchen paper on the surface of the mince. The paper will soak up the fat, but the non-fat

juices will quickly run off.

Now use this mince to make Shepherd's or Cottage Pie.

PROPER SHEPHERD'S PIE

'There's much debate about what constitutes Cottage Pie or Shepherd's Pie,' says Prue Leith. 'I guess Shepherd's would be made of lamb or mutton and Cottage with beef.'

Anyway, the best consists of Basic Mince plus 225 g/8 oz quartered fried mushrooms and a teaspoon of fresh thyme. And the potato is nearly as important as the meat. Allow 450 g/1 lb of fluffy 'baking type' potatoes per person. Peel and boil fast until completely tender. Push through a vegetable mouli or mincer (*not* a processor, which will make them into glue) rather than bashing with a 'masher'. Mashers never quite get all the lumps out. For every 450 g/1 lb of potato, add 75 g/3 oz butter. But not milk. Season with salt and pepper. Spread while warm on to the cold meat mixture. The perfect proportions are 50% mince and 50% potato. Mark the top of the mash with a fork. Sprinkle with breadcrumbs and then milk and butter.

To reheat (and brown the top) put in a moderate oven (180°C, 350°F, Gas Mark 4) for 40 minutes.

LEFT Proper shepherd's pie

from JEREMY ROUND
MANTI
(Turkish lamb dumplings)

This adaptation of a Turkish recipe for lamb, rather like ravioli, comes from JEREMY ROUND of *The Independent*. He says it is best made with slightly maturer meat from British lambs offered for sale in the period January to March, although it also works well with younger animals.

200 g/7 oz plain flour
½ teaspoon salt
1 egg (size 3), beaten
about 4 tablespoons water
225 g/8 oz lean minced lamb
2 shallots, peeled and finely chopped
1 tablespoon finely chopped parsley
½ teaspoon ground cumin
salt and black pepper
150 ml/¼ pint strained Greek yogurt
1 garlic clove, peeled and crushed
40 g/1½ oz butter
½ teaspoon cayenne pepper

First make the pasta dough. Sift the flour and salt into a pile on your work surface. Make a well in the top and pour in the egg and half the water. With your finger tips, or using a fork, mix the liquid while gradually drawing in the flour until a medium-firm dough is formed, adding the rest of the water if necessary. The exact amount of flour and water you need will vary according to the flour itself, the humidity of the room and the freshness of the eggs. Judge that the consistency is right by sticking your finger in. It should go in fairly easily and come out clean, with no stickiness. Form into a ball.

With clean, dry hands, knead the dough on a lightly floured surface by holding the edge of ball nearest you with the fingers of one hand, while you push the rest of the ball away with the heel of the other hand. Then roll the extended edge back toward you with the palm of that hand. Turn the dough through 90 degrees and repeat. At first it

will stick and tear. Persevere (lightly flouring hands and board as necessary) until it is quite elastic and you can stretch it a long way across the work surface. This will take about 10 minutes.

Form the dough into a ball once more. Its surface should have a silky texture like a baby's cheek. Cover the ball in cling film and leave to rest at room temperature for at least 1 hour (3 hours at most).

Unwrap, knead again for a minute or two, and place on a large, immaculately clean, dry surface, sprinkled with very little flour. Very lightly push a floured rolling pin across the top of the dough away from you. Turn dough through 90 degrees and repeat. Continue working, exerting almost no pressure at all downwards, and only rolling away from you, until you can see the work surface through the sheet. Cut this extremely thin, translucent sheet into 5 cm/2 inch squares.

Now preheat the oven to moderately hot (190°C, 375°F, Gas Mark 5).

Mix the lamb, shallots, parsley and cumin thoroughly with salt and pepper to taste. Put 1 teaspoon of the meat mixture into the centre of each pasta square, wet the inside edges of the squares and draw up the four corners together into the middle, sealing together along the wet edges so that the whole top side of the dumpling is in the form of a raised cross.

Arrange the finished dumplings in a single layer in a buttered baking dish (they can be packed quite closely). Bake, uncovered, in the preheated oven for 25–30 minutes until coloured. Swish in water to half the depth of the manti. Cover with foil and return to the oven for 15 minutes.

Beat the yogurt with the garlic and a good sprinkling of salt. Pour over the manti. Melt the butter in a small saucepan. When foaming, mix in the cayenne. Pour this mixture, while it is still sizzling, over the yogurt.

Serve immediately. Diners should spoon out their own portions of yogurt and butter-covered dumplings into their own

bowls with a little of the cooking liquid. Eat the manti while they are hot.

These manti will not keep, freeze or microwave.

SERVES 2–4

from CHRISTENA APPLEYARD
SPICY PORK CHOPS

CHRISTENA APPLEYARD, Woman's Editor of the *Daily Mirror*, provided this tangy recipe for pork. It would also work well with fillet, rather than chops.

4 large pork chops

Marinade
2 tablespoons oil
1 garlic clove, peeled and chopped
1 tablespoon Worcester sauce
2 tablespoons soy sauce
1 tablespoon tomato purée
1 tablespoon wine vinegar
1 tablespoon dried ginger
1–2 tablespoons chilli sauce
freshly ground black pepper

Mix together the ingredients for the marinade, add the chops and coat them thoroughly. Marinate overnight.

Next day, remove the chops from the marinade and grill under a preheated hot grill. Baste continually with the marinade until it is used up.

SERVES 4

RIGHT Manti

from EVELYN ROSE
GUISADO CON CIRUELAS
(*Spanish beef with prunes*)

EVELYN ROSE, food writer and broadcaster and Consumer Commissioner on the Meat and Livestock Commission, provides a dash of the exotic with this recipe, in which chunky pieces of beef are stewed in spiced white wine. Prunes are an unexpected addition.

1.25 kg/2½ lb top rib or good stewing beef, trimmed and cut into 5 cm/2 inch chunks
2 tablespoons plain flour, seasoned with 2 teaspoons salt and 15 grinds black pepper
3 tablespoons olive oil
1 large onion, peeled and finely sliced
1 garlic clove, peeled and finely chopped
1 teaspoon dark brown sugar
150 ml/¼ pint fairly dry white wine
2 tablespoons tomato purée
300 ml/½ pint boiling water plus 1 meat stock cube, or 300 ml/½ pint thin beef gravy
1 teaspoon paprika
225 g/8 oz ready-pitted prunes, or 225g/8 oz regular prunes, soaked in strained tea overnight before stoning
26 g/1 oz toasted pine kernels (optional, but delicious)

Preheat the oven to cool (150°C, 300°F, Gas Mark 2).

Put the seasoned flour in a plastic bag, add the beef cubes in two portions, and shake until evenly coated.

Heat 2 tablespoons of the oil in a large pan and brown the meat in it in two portions until a rich brown on all sides, then lift on to a plate lined with absorbent kitchen paper.

Add the remaining oil to the pan, if necessary, then gently cook the onion and garlic, covering the pan for 5 minutes then uncovering and sprinkling with the brown sugar. Continue to cook until golden brown.

Add the wine and bubble for a minute or 2, then add all the remaining ingredients except the pine kernels, stirring, and bring to the boil.

Put the beef into an ovenproof casserole and pour on the sauce, which should barely cover the meat. If it does not, add a little boiling water.

Cover and cook in the preheated oven for 2½–3 hours, making sure the liquid is barely bubbling. Turn the oven down if the casserole is cooking too quickly. After 2 hours, add a little boiling liquid, if necessary: the sauce should be thick but still very juicy.

Taste the casserole at this point and adjust the seasoning, if necessary.

Meanwhile, put the pine kernels on a heatproof dish and leave in the oven until golden brown, or toss over direct heat in a non-stick frying pan.

Garnish each serving of beef with a sprinkling of the pine kernels.

SERVES 6

from DON PHILPOTT
STEAK DIANE WITH RÖSTI POTATOES

DON PHILPOTT, who is the food and drink correspondent of the *Press Association* and travels extensively in Europe and beyond, likes this lovely combination of dishes, because it is easy and quick to prepare but spectacular in the final preparation and serving. 'It is an easy dish, but you must use best quality meat,' says Don.

750 g–1 kg/1½–2 lbs rump or fillet steak (depending on appetites)
100 g/4 oz unsalted butter
2 large shallots, peeled and finely chopped
4 teaspoons caster sugar
grated rind and juice of 2 lemons
½ teaspoon Worcestershire sauce
120 ml/4 fl oz brandy
chopped parsley, to garnish

Rösti potatoes
1 kg/2 lb potatoes, peeled
75–100 g/3–4 oz unsalted butter
1 teaspoon salt
black pepper
½ teaspoon chopped fresh parsley

Start preparing the Rösti potatoes the day before. Warm the potatoes, put them in a saucepan, cover with cold water and boil for between 5–7 minutes until they are just turning soft. Drain and leave overnight, then strain and grate coarsely.

When ready to cook the recipe, trim and cut the steak into equal-size pieces and beat flat with the flat side of a meat tenderizer, hammer or rolling pin until they are about 5 mm/¼ inch thick.

Now start cooking the potatoes. Melt the butter in a large skillet. Add the grated potatoes, sprinkle with salt and season with pepper and parsley. Fry over a gentle heat for about 15 minutes, turning the potatoes to ensure they do not turn too brown. Use a spatula to press down on the potatoes to form a pancake and allow the bottom to crisp and brown.

Melt the butter for the steaks in a large, heavy-based pan, and fry the shallots until soft. Remove and keep hot.

Raise the heat and fry the steaks for about 1 minute on each side to seal the surface. Remove and keep hot. Add extra butter as necessary until all the steaks have been treated in this way.

Return the shallots to the pan, stir in the sugar, lemon rind, juice and Worcestershire sauce. Return the steaks, pour over the brandy, pre-warmed in a small saucepan over a flame, and flambé. Serve immediately, still flaming if possible, and with the potato 'pancake' turned out on to a warmed dish so that the brown crispy side is on top.

SERVES 4

LEFT Steak Diane with rösti potatoes

from SUE CARROLL
POT ROAST PORK WITH AUBERGINE

SUE CARROLL, Woman's Editor of the *Sun*, likes the tasty combination of pork, aubergine and other vegetables in this easy-to-prepare casserole.

1.5 kg/3 lb leg of pork, boned and rolled
salt and black pepper
2 tablespoons oil
3 onions, peeled and cut into wedges
300 ml/½ pint beef stock
1 tablespoon Worcestershire sauce
½ teaspoon ground coriander
1 large aubergine, trimmed, halved
    lengthways and sliced
2 large carrots, peeled and sliced

To garnish
baked tomatoes
continental parsley

Preheat the oven to moderately hot (190°C, 375°F, Gas Mark 5).

Sprinkle the pork with salt and pepper. Heat the oil in a frying pan and fry the pork all over until browned. Transfer to a casserole.

Fry the onions in the same fat for 1 minute, then arrange round the pork.

Combine the stock and Worcestershire sauce, add plenty of salt and pepper and the coriander. Pour over the joint and cover the casserole. Put into the preheated oven and cook for 1 hour.

Baste the joint, add the aubergine and carrots to the casserole, cover and return to the oven for a further 1–1¼ hours, or until tender.

Remove the meat to a serving dish and arrange the drained vegetables around it.

Remove any fat from the surface of the pan juices, taste and adjust the seasoning and pour into a jug to serve with the pork. Garnish the joint with baked tomatoes and continental parsley, if available. Otherwise use English parsley.

SERVES 6

Pot roast pork with aubergine

from LIS LEIGH
GRILLED CALF'S LIVER WITH LIME

This recipe was given to LIS LEIGH, *Sunday Times* Food and Drink Correspondent, by Pierre Koffman for her book *The Sunday Times Guide to Enlightened Eating*, published by Century Hutchinson in 1986.

Grilled calf's liver with lime

4 thick slices calf's liver
1 tablespoon caster sugar
2 tablespoons wine vinegar
juice of ½ lemon
juice of 1 orange
250 ml/8 fl oz chicken stock
2 shallots, peeled and chopped
1 knob butter (optional)
1 lime, quartered

To prepare the sauce, put the sugar and vinegar in a heavy saucepan and mix together. Cook until the mixture caramelizes, then add the lemon juice, orange juice, chicken stock and chopped shallots. Boil until the liquid is reduced by half. Add a knob of butter if required.

Grill the liver pieces for 2 minutes on each side so they remain pink inside. To serve, pour the sauce over the liver and use the lime quarters as a garnish. Serve the finished dish with rice and a fresh green vegetable.

SERVES 4

from JOHN DUNN
PORK AND KIDNEY COBBLER

JOHN DUNN, *Radio 2* presenter, offers this hearty dish as ideal for an autumn or winter meal.

450 g/1 lb cubed pork
2 lamb's kidneys, skinned, cored and cut
*   into 4*
25 g/1 oz plain seasoned flour
1 tablespoon oil
16 button onions, or 1 large onion, peeled
*   and sliced*
2 carrots, sliced
2 teaspoons paprika
450 g/1 lb tomatoes, peeled, seeded and
*   chopped*
300 ml/½ pint hot stock
100 g/4 oz button mushrooms

Scone topping
50 g/2 oz margarine
225 g/8 oz plain flour
1 tablespoon baking powder
salt
4 tablespoons milk, buttermilk or plain
*   unsweetened yogurt*
1 teaspoon caraway seeds

Preheat the oven to moderate (160°C, 325°F, Gas Mark 3).

Coat the pork and kidneys with seasoned flour. Heat the oil and brown the meat, a few pieces at a time, then transfer to a casserole dish. Lightly brown the onions and carrots and add to the casserole. Stir in the paprika, remaining flour, tomatoes and stock.

Cover the casserole and cook in the centre of the preheated oven for one hour.

Meanwhile, make the topping: rub the margarine into the flour, baking powder and salt. Add the milk or yogurt to make a soft dough. Roll out and cut into about 12 rounds using a 5 cm/2 inch biscuit cutter. Remove the casserole from the oven and increase the heat to hot (200°C, 400°F, Gas Mark 6). Add the mushrooms to the casserole. Arrange the scones on top, brush them with a little milk, sprinkle with the caraway seeds and bake, uncovered, for 15–20 minutes.

Illustrated on page 73   SERVES 4

from JIMMY YOUNG
HAND-RAISED PORK PIES

This fine, simple version for the traditional British pork pie comes from Radio 2 broadcaster and personality JIMMY YOUNG.

Hot water crust pastry
500 g/1¼ lb plain flour
250 ml/8 fl oz water
225 ml/8 oz lard

1.5 kg/3 lb pork shoulder, finely chopped
1 teaspoon chopped parsley
salt and black pepper
milk to glaze
150 ml/¼ pint jellied stock, made from pork
*   bones*

Preheat the oven to moderately hot (190°C, 350°F, Gas Mark 5).

To make the hot water crust pastry, sieve the flour into a bowl and make a well in the centre. Heat the lard and water in a pan until just boiling, tip in the flour, and mix well with a wooden spoon. When the mixture has cooled slightly, turn out and knead until the pastry is smooth.

Cut off a quarter of the pastry and return this to the warm pan. Flatten out the remaining pastry into 4 large thick rounds. Place a 1 kg/2 lb jam jar in the centre of each and work the pastry up the sides. Allow to cool and remove the jam jar. It is essential to work quickly as the lard soon sets, making the pastry brittle. (If you preferred, you could use a small cake tin or pie mould to shape the pastry.)

Mix together the pork, parsley and seasoning and put in the pastry cases. Roll out the remaining pastry to form lids and place on top of the pies. Seal the edges well and glaze with milk. Make a hole in the centre of each pie.

Place the pies on a baking sheet low in the preheated oven and cook for about 2 hours. If they become too brown, cover them with foil.

When cooked and cooled, pour in the jellied stock through a funnel. If desired, a pastry rose which has been baked separately can be placed in the centre of each pie, to conceal the hole.

MAKES 4 PIES

RIGHT Hand-raised pork pies

from MATTHEW KELLY
PORK WITH PRUNES

Combining pork and prunes is a classic way of cooking this meat. It is one which is much appreciated by TV personality and actor MATTHEW KELLY, who contributed this splendid version using fillet of pork.

2 pork fillets, about 750 g/1½ lb
salt and black pepper

Stuffing
50 g/2 oz stoned prunes, soaked overnight
*   and chopped*
50 g/2 oz fresh breadcrumbs
1 small onion, peeled and finely chopped
½ teaspoon dried thyme
1 egg yolk

2 tablespoons vegetable oil
1 onion, peeled and chopped
150 ml/¼ pint beef stock
4 tablespoons white wine
100 g/4 oz stoned prunes, soaked overnight
2 tablespoons brandy (optional)
3–4 tablespoons double cream
sprigs of fresh herbs or parsley, to garnish

Preheat the oven to moderate (180°C, 350°F, Gas Mark 4).

Split the pork fillets open a little with a sharp knife and season lightly.

To make the stuffing, mix the prunes, breadcrumbs, onion, thyme, salt and pepper, then bind together with the egg yolk. Spread over 1 piece of pork, cover with the second piece and secure with string.

Heat the oil in a pan and fry the piece of pork until browned all over. Transfer to a shallow ovenproof dish.

Fry the onion in the same fat until lightly browned. Drain off all the fat, then add the stock, wine, prunes and plenty of salt and pepper to the pan and bring to the boil.

Warm the brandy (if using), pour over the pork and ignite carefully. Pour the sauce over and around the pork and cover the dish with a lid or foil.

Transfer it to the preheated oven and cook for about 1 hour, or until tender.

Remove the pork from the oven dish, take off the string and slice the meat. Add the cream to the sauce, adjust the seasoning and replace the pork in the sauce. Garnish with sprigs of fresh herbs.

SERVES 4

from GLORIA HUNNIFORD
LAMB LOIN CHOPS WITH CHILLI BEANS

Radio personality and television chat-show hostess GLORIA HUNNIFORD likes the spicy texture of this delicious recipe for lamb which uses the lean cuts of loin chops or leg steaks in tandem with red kidney beans and spices.

4 lamb loin chops or leg steaks
1 tablespoon corn or sunflower oil
1 onion, peeled and chopped
1 × 200 g/7 oz can tomatoes
1 × 400 g/14 oz can red kidney beans,
*   drained and rinsed*
2 tablespoons tomato purée
1 teaspoon chilli powder
1 teaspoon cumin
1 teaspoon sugar
salt

Brush the chops lightly with oil and cook under a pre-heated grill on a medium heat.

Meanwhile, heat the oil and fry the onion until soft. Add the remaining ingredients and bring to the boil. Simmer for 10 minutes. Serve with the chops and with wholewheat pasta.

SERVES 4

LEFT Pork with prunes;
BELOW Lamb loin chops with chilli beans

from CLAIRE RAYNER
PORK AND VEGETABLE LAYER

Here is a delicious pork and vegetable dish from writer, novelist and broadcaster CLAIRE RAYNER.

350 g/12 oz lean shoulder pork, cubed
2 teaspoons seasoned plain flour
25 g/1 oz butter or margarine
1 garlic clove, peeled and finely chopped
1 onion, peeled and sliced
1 × 425 g/15 oz can tomatoes
½ teaspoon sweet basil
½ chicken stock cube
salt and black pepper
750 g/1½ lb courgettes, thinly sliced
50 g/2 oz Cheddar cheese, grated
50 g/2 oz fresh brown breadcrumbs

Preheat the oven to moderate (180°C, 350°F, Gas Mark 4).

Toss the pork in the flour. Melt the butter or margarine, add the garlic and brown the pork. Reserve on a plate.

Place the sliced onion, tomatoes with their juice, basil and the stock cube in a frying pan and bring to the boil. Add any remaining flour and stir until thickened. Season to taste.

Grease the base of a shallow ovenproof dish. Layer half the sliced courgettes over the base of the dish. Place the pork cubes evenly over the courgettes and then cover with the tomato and onion mixture. Layer the remaining courgette slices over the pork and tomato mixture. Mix together the cheese and breadcrumbs and sprinkle over the top of the courgettes.

Bake in the preheated oven for 1½ hours, until the topping is golden brown and the meat is cooked.

Serve the dish hot, perhaps with potatoes baked in the oven while the pork dish is cooking.

SERVES 4

from ADRIAN LOVE
COLD ROAST LOIN OF PORK WITH SPICY FRUIT STUFFING

This recipe for cold pork, ideal for summer eating, comes from *Radio 2* presenter ADRIAN LOVE.

Stuffing

1 eating apple, peeled, cored and chopped
100 g/4 oz dried apricots, soaked overnight.
50 g/2 oz pine nuts
1 teaspoon ground coriander
½ teaspoon ground cumin
salt and black pepper

1.5 kg/3 lb boned loin of pork, rind removed
2 garlic cloves, peeled and sliced
salt and black pepper

Preheat the oven to moderate (180°C, 350°F, Gas Mark 4).

To make the stuffing, chop the fruit and mix with the pine nuts. Mix in the spices and seasoning. Spread the stuffing over the pork, roll and tie with string.

Using the point of a sharp knife, make small incisions all over the joint and insert a sliver of garlic into each. Season the joint with salt and pepper.

Weigh the joint and calculate the cooking time: allow 30 minutes per 450 g/1 lb, plus 30 minutes.

Cook on a rack in the centre of the pre-heated oven.

When the joint is cooked, remove from the oven and allow to cool. Serve cold, thinly sliced, with a selection of salads.

SERVES 6–8

RIGHT Pork and kidney cobbler (see page 68)

from MIKE OWEN
THREE-FILLET ROAST

MIKE OWEN, Programme Controller with *BRMB* radio in Birmingham, has broadcast several food and cooking series, one with John Tovey, well-known restaurateur, hotelier and cookery writer and broadcaster. Mike Owen admires John Tovey for his creative approach to his art in general and for this clever and impressive way with meat fillets in particular. (The recipe was published in *The Miller Howe Cookbook* by Century Hutchinson, 1988.)

'When carved, the roast looks impressive on the plate and creates some surprise to have the three tastes (four including the bacon) combined in this clever way. It never fails to create a reaction – always positive,' says Mike.

450 g/1 lb smoked bacon
750 g/1½ lb fillet of beef, about 25 cm/10 inches long
225 g/8 oz fillet of pork, about 20 cm/8 inches long
2 lamb fillets, about 75–100 g/3–4 oz each

Preheat the oven to hot (220°C, 425°F, Gas Mark 7).

Arrange the slices of bacon on a work top, thin ends to the centre, fat ends to the outside. This is to be the 'overcoat' for the roast. Place the beef fillet in the middle and place the pork fillet along the top of this, with the two lamb fillets alongside. You should have a sausage-shape from the four pieces of meat. Bring over the thick ends of bacon, creating a bacon lattice cover. Use cocktail sticks to hold the shape together.

Place the roast in a roasting dish in the pre-heated oven and cook for 45–60 minutes, depending on taste.

Once cooked, transfer the roast to a warmed serving plate and remove the cocktail sticks. Carve it in thin or thick slices, as you prefer.

SERVES 4

from NEIL FOX
CONTINENTAL SHEPHERD'S PIE

NEIL FOX, *DJ* with Capital Radio in London, is a keen cook and often adapts traditional recipes to suit himself. He likes to make things that are quick, easy and tasty. This recipe makes a super lunch or supper dish, says Neil; his friends call it their Foxy Favourite!

450 g/1 lb minced beef
2 tablespoons oil (optional: see below)
1 large onion, peeled and chopped
3 large carrots, scrubbed and sliced
1 courgette, sliced
½ aubergine, sliced
1 garlic clove, peeled and sliced
1 × 400 g/14 oz can chopped tomatoes
1 × 400 g/14 oz can red kidney beans,
  drained
900 g/2 lb potatoes, peeled
salt and black pepper
1 large knob of butter
150 ml/¼ pint milk
50 g/2 oz grated Cheddar cheese

Preheat the oven to moderate (160°C, 325°F, Gas Mark 3).

If the mince seems quite fatty, 'render' it in a saucepan first and transfer it to an ovenproof casserole with a slotted spoon. Into the beef fat (adding the oil if the beef is very lean) put the chopped onion, sliced carrots, courgette, aubergine and garlic and simmer until soft, turning frequently.

Tip the vegetables into the casserole with the mince, pour the tomatoes then the drained kidney beans on top and cover the casserole. Cook in the preheated oven for 20–25 minutes.

Put the potatoes into a saucepan of salted cold water and bring them to the boil, cooking them until they are soft. Drain and mash them with the butter and milk, return to the heat and stir until the butter melts and the milk has heated through.

LEFT Continental shepherd's pie

Take the meat mixture from the oven, add salt and pepper, if necessary. Put the mashed potato over the top of the meat mixture and sprinkle the grated cheese over it. Pop under a hot grill until the cheese melts and turns golden brown.

Serve this with either large chunks of fresh wholemeal bread and butter or a green salad.

SERVES 4

from MARY BERRY
PORK STIR-FRY

'English pork fillet is an excellent buy, being lean, tender and taking just a short time to cook', says TV cook MARY BERRY, whose stir-fry recipe here is very popular with her family. 'The meat is best sliced in thin strips for this stir-fry. It helps to part-freeze the fillet for about 30 minutes in the freezer to make the flesh firmer to cut. Prepare all the ingredients and assemble them together, then fry at the very last moment. In the summer we sometimes stir-fry in an old wok in the hot embers of the barbecue in the garden.'

1 pork fillet, about 275 g/10 oz
350 g/12 oz white cabbage
6 spring onions
2 teaspoons cornflour
2 tablespoons sherry
about 2 tablespoons olive oil
salt and black pepper
1 red pepper, seeded and sliced
350 g/12 oz fresh beansprouts
1 fat garlic clove, peeled and crushed
100 ml/3½ fl oz good stock
2 tablespoons soy sauce

Trim off any surplus skin or fat from the fillet (there will be very little). Slice the pork into fine pencil-thin strips. Shred the cabbage finely. Cut each spring onion into about 6 pieces, cutting diagonally. Blend

the cornflour with the sherry in a small bowl and set aside.

Heat the oil in a wok or deepish large frying pan until very hot. Season the pork and cook for 2 minutes, tossing with two wooden spatulas all the time. Lift out and keep on one side.

Reheat the pan, adding a little more oil if needed, and add the cabbage, spring onions, red pepper, beansprouts and garlic. Cook for about 3–4 minutes, tossing all the time. Return the pork to the pan and stir in the stock, soy sauce and sherry mixture. Cook for a further minute until the liquid has thickened slightly and the vegetables are still crisp. Taste and check seasoning. Serve at once.

SERVES 4

from FRED DINENAGE
BOEUF BOURGUIGNONNE

This recipe comes from FRED DINENAGE, presenter of *TVS*'s *'Coast to Coast'*. It is his favourite on two counts – it is quite delicious, and it is, he says, just about the only thing he is able to cook successfully. Another reason he likes it is that it contains a reasonable amount of good, cheap red wine!

750 g/1½ lb chuck steak or top leg of beef
25 g/1 oz bacon fat or dripping
175 g/6 oz streaky bacon
1 tablespoon plain flour
300 ml/½ pint water
1 beef stock cube
150 ml/¼ pint cheap red wine
bay leaf
½ teaspoon dried mixed herbs
sprig parsley
about ½ teaspoon salt
dash of pepper
12 baby onions, peeled

Preheat the oven to very moderate (160°C, 325°F, Gas Mark 3).

Cut the steak in 4 cm/1½ inch cubes. Derind and chop the bacon. Melt the fat or dripping in a fairly large pan and crisp the bacon in it. Remove the bacon and place in a 3-pint ovenproof casserole. Fry the steak in the fat remaining in the pan until it is golden brown. Transfer it to the casserole.

Pour away most of the fat in the pan, leaving about 2 tablespoons. Blend in the flour and cook until browned. Stir in the stock and wine. Bring this sauce to boiling point and simmer until thickened, then stir in the bay leaf, herbs, parsley and seasoning. Pour this liquor over the meat, cover and transfer to the preheated oven. Cook for 1½ hours.

Add the onions to the casserole and cook for a further hour, or until the meat is really tender. Add more seasoning if necessary. Skim off any excess fat before serving.

SERVES 4

from SUE KING
SHEPHERD'S PIE WITH A DIFFERENCE

Television South West presenter and journalist SUE KING shares her favourite quick and easy informal dinner party dish. It is a favourite with her friends. Not only is it quick and tasty, it's economic and healthy, with the substitution of the carrot and swede for the more traditional potato.

1 kg/2 lb minced beef
1 large onion, peeled and chopped
1 garlic clove, peeled and crushed
brown sauce (to taste)
tomato purée (to taste)
1 small tin of tomatoes
small quantity beef stock
touch of cornflour, to thicken
salt and black pepper
750 g/1½ lb carrots, boiled and mashed
2 large swedes, boiled and mashed
100 g/4 oz grated cheese

Boil the minced beef, to eliminate excess fat. Drain and set aside.

Fry the onion and garlic in a little cooking oil until semi-cooked. Add the minced beef, brown sauce, tomato purée, tomatoes, salt and pepper, beef stock and a touch of cornflour to thicken the mixture.

When well cooked, transfer to a large oven-proof dish. Boil the carrot and swede separately until soft. Drain and mash. Spread a layer of mashed carrot on the minced beef mixture, then top the carrot with mashed swede. Cook in a preheated moderate oven (180°C, 350°F, Gas Mark 4) for 20 minutes. Top the pie with the grated cheese and finish off under a hot grill.

SERVES 4

from GRACE MULLIGAN
PORKY CHESTNUTS

Among the hundreds of recipes collected by GRACE MULLIGAN over her years of presenting television's longest-running cookery programme, *Farmhouse Kitchen* on Yorkshire Television, this one stands out as a particularly good one for pork. She says, 'Remember to soak the chestnuts overnight, and to clean off any brown skin still sticking to them.'

225 g/8 oz pork fillet or tenderloin
2 tablespoons vegetable oil
1 medium-sized onion, peeled and sliced
1 medium-sized eating apple, peeled, cored and chopped
150 g/6 oz dried chestnuts, soaked
300 ml/½ pint apple juice
300 ml/½ pint light stock
½ teaspoon oregano
25 g/1 oz plain flour
100 g/4 oz firm mushrooms, sliced
15 g/½ oz butter
25 g/1 oz dark raisins

Preheat the oven to moderately hot (200°C, 400°F, Gas Mark 6).

Trim the pork and cut it into 2 cm/¾ inch cubes.

Heat half the oil and fry the pork briskly on all sides for 2–3 minutes. Transfer to a roomy casserole.

Use the remaining oil to fry the onion until it is just beginning to brown.

Strain the cooked onion and add it to the casserole with the apples and the drained chestnuts. Sprinkle over the flour and stir it in until smooth.

Stir in the apple juice, stock and oregano. Cover and cook in a preheated oven for about 40–45 minutes.

Ten minutes before the end of the cooking time, lightly cook the mushrooms in the butter. Stir the mushrooms and raisins into the casserole and re-heat.

SERVES 4

from SUE AMODIO AND
DAVE BROWN
BEEF AND ORANGE CARBONADE

This recipe was cooked by SUE AMODIO, with DAVE BROWN, on the Great Yarmouth and Norwich local radio station *Radio Broadland*. It should be prepared and cooked the day before you intend serving it to allow the flavours to blend and mature well.

Beef and orange carbonade

25 g/1 oz butter
1 tablespoon vegetable oil
750–900 g/1½ lb–2 lb braising or stewing
    steak, in large pieces
1 medium onion, peeled and chopped
2 garlic cloves, peeled and chopped
100 g/4 oz carrots, sliced thickly
100 g/4 oz turnips, cut into chunks
2 sticks celery, chopped
2 tablespoons plain flour
2 bay leaves
2 teaspoons nutmeg
300 ml/½ pint brown ale
150 ml/¼ pint beef stock
1 tablespoon tomato purée
salt and black pepper
100 g/4 oz mushrooms, sliced
grated rind and juice of 2 oranges
orange twists

Heat the butter and oil in a large flameproof casserole or saucepan. Add the meat in batches and brown well on all sides. Remove with a slotted spoon.

Add the vegetables to the casserole and fry until lightly browned. Sprinkle in the flour and spices and stir well. Gradually add the brown ale, stock, tomato purée and seasoning and bring to the boil, stirring.

Return the meat carefully to the casserole, cover tightly and simmer gently for 2 hours on top of the stove, or in an oven preheated to moderate (160°C, 325°F, Gas Mark 3) for about 2½ hours. Stir in the mushrooms and the orange rind and juice.

The next day, reheat the carbonade for 40 minutes. Remove the bay leaves before serving, garnished with orange twists.

SERVES 4

from SUSAN BROOKES
BEEF AND HAM IN PARCELS

SUSAN BROOKES, cookery programme
presenter for *Granada Television*, says this
recipe can be 'tarted up' for a dinner party
by adding a dessertspoonful of brandy to
each parcel.

50 g/2 oz butter
100 g/4 oz mushrooms, sliced
1 medium onion, peeled and chopped
4 portions of beef fillet, cut as thick as you
  can afford
4 slices of ham, same size as fillets of beef
salt and black pepper

Preheat the oven to hot (220°C, 425°F, Gas
Mark 7).
   Melt the butter in a frying pan, and
gently fry the mushrooms and onion in it
for a couple of minutes.
   Take 4 pieces of baking foil, each big
enough to enclose one piece of meat. Put a
piece of fillet steak in the centre of a piece of
foil, a piece of ham on top, and a quarter of
the onion and mushroom mixture on each.
Season to taste with salt and pepper, and
wrap each 'parcel' firmly but not too tightly
– you can make a shape rather like a cornish
pastry. Cook in the preheated oven for 20
minutes.

SERVES 4

Beef and ham in parcels

from STEVE COLMAN
YUM YUM I'LL HAVE MORE OF THAT

This tangy way with sirloin steak is the suggestion of STEVE COLMAN, Breakfast DJ with *Metro Radio*, Newcastle upon Tyne.

1 × 1 kg/2 lb piece of sirloin steak
4 tablespoons of French mustard
1 full branch of fresh tarragon – chopped
salt and black pepper
1 garlic clove, peeled
50 g/2 oz butter
1 medium-sized pot double cream
few splashes whisky or brandy

Mix the tarragon with 2 tablespoons of the mustard and spread over the steak, kneading in all over. Leave for an hour or so.

Melt the butter in a frying pan with the garlic clove, add the steak and seal over a high heat then continue cooking on a lower heat for a quarter of an hour or so – if you like yours rare, do it for less time. Remove the meat to a separate serving dish and keep hot.

Put the remaining mustard and half the cream into the pan with the meat juices; heat slowly until it is quite hot, then add the rest of the cream and splash in the whisky or brandy to taste. Slice the steak into your required sizes and dollop the sauce all over.

The steak is good served with stuffed tomatoes, baby corn, and boiled potatoes.
SERVES 3–4

NOTE: if you have it, you could use ready-made tarragon mustard instead of the French mustard and fresh tarragon. This would give the flavour of tarragon in the sauce as well as the meat, of course.

Yum yum I'll have more of that

from PAUL FROST
FROSTY'S LAMB KEBABS

PAUL FROST, of *Tyne Tees Television's Northern Life* programme, often serves these kebabs, with their delicious tang of Indian cookery.

ABOVE Frosty's lamb kebabs

225–250 g/8–9 oz lamb fillet, shoulder or
   leg
4 tablespoons plain yogurt
1½ tablespoons lemon juice
1 × 2.5 cm/1 inch cube of fresh ginger,
   peeled and finely grated
1 small green chilli, seeded and very finely
   chopped
1 garlic clove, peeled and mashed to a pulp
1 teaspoon ground cumin seeds
½ teaspoon ground coriander seeds
½ teaspoon cayenne pepper
¾ teaspoon salt
black pepper
vegetable oil

Cut the meat into good-sized cubes and place in a glass or china bowl.
   Put the yogurt, lemon juice, ginger,

chilli, garlic, cumin, coriander, cayenne, salt and pepper in a bowl and mix well. Pour the yogurt mixture through a sieve on to the meat, pushing it through the sieve to extract all the paste you can. Mix the meat and the marinade well, cover and put in the refrigerator for 6–24 hours.
   Next day, remove the meat from the marinade and thread it on to skewers, balancing the filled skewers across the edges of a baking dish or grill pan so that the meat juices drip inside. Brush the kebabs generously with oil and place under the grill. When one side of the meat is brown turn the skewers over, making sure to brush the meat with more oil before pushing it back under the grill.
   Serve with thick slices of lemon.

SERVES

COMPETITION WINNERS
AROUND BRITAIN

Some of our top circulation regional news-papers ran a series of competitions to find the most delicious and appealing recipes combining local ingredients with the best of British meat. This chapter contains some of the best competition winners from around the country.

from LINDA HORNZEE-JONES
DEVILLED KIDNEY SANDWICH, OR SOME-LIKE-IT-HOT

LINDA HORNZEE-JONES won the *Croydon Advertiser* recipe competition with this deceptively simple recipe for kidneys. She says it is guaranteed to cure a head cold!

2 pig's kidneys, or 4 lamb's kidneys
2 thick-cut slices wholemeal bread
creamed horseradish sauce

Halve, trim and core the kidneys (and slice again horizontally if too thick).

Under a very hot grill, toast *one* side only of the bread, and grill the kidneys until firm.

Spread the untoasted sides of the bread with horseradish sauce (no butter – just 'butter' the bread with the sauce).

Sandwich the cooked kidneys between the sauced bread and eat them while they are very hot.

SERVES 1

from MARJORIE JONES
BOOZY COCKLED BEEF

MARJORIE JONES' recipe for beef stuffed with cockles won for her the *Manchester Evening News* competition.

750 g/1½ lb stewing or braising steak, in one thick and even piece
1 bottle stout
3 pickling onions, peeled and finely chopped
4 medium-sized potatoes, peeled and sliced
2 carrots, slivered
½ small swede, cubed
½ small turnip, cubed
300 ml/½ pint hot beef stock
1 tablespoon Worcester sauce
100 g/4 oz cockles
50 g/2 oz dried apricots, chopped
1 tablespoon green peppercorns
½ teaspoon powdered rosemary
salt and black pepper
French mustard
vegetable oil
1 tablespoon chopped walnuts

Marinate the beef in the stout for 3 hours or, preferably, overnight.

Preheat the oven to moderately hot (200°C, 400°F, Gas Mark 6).

Put the onions, potatoes, carrots, swede, turnip, beef stock and Worcester sauce in a deep casserole dish. Put a wire grid over the vegetables so the meat will not touch them.

Remove the beef from the marinade and cut a pocket into it. Mix together the cockles, apricots, peppercorns, rosemary and seasoning and use to fill the pocket in the beef. Skewer or sew up the pocket.

Place the steak on the grid in the casserole and brush with French mustard and oil. Cover the casserole and cook in the preheated oven for 20 minutes. Reduce the oven to moderate (160°C, 325°F, Gas Mark 3) and continue to cook the casserole for about 1 hour, or until the meat is tender. Remove the meat from the casserole and take out the skewer or string.

Put the steak on a warmed serving dish and sprinkle with the walnuts. Remove the vegetables from the casserole and put them round the meat. The gravy can be thickened and served separately.

Illustrated on page 82 SERVES 4

from JOAN BUSH
BARD'S SPECIAL

JOAN BUSH won the *Coventry Evening Telegraph's* competition with the recipe for the pork and apricot pie she always serves on Shakespeare's birthday. As she says, although this is in late April, the weather is not always very springlike and after a morning outside watching the Birthday procession through Stratford upon Avon and the country dancing in chilly winds, the pie is a good, warming dish to come home to.

She usually buys her meat from her favourite butcher in Chipping Campden. 'He always buys the best meat at the market, so it is super,' she says. She serves Bard's Special with a salad of watercress, celery and chopped walnuts from the tree in her own garden in Stratford upon Avon.

100 g/4 oz dried apricots
450 g/1 lb pork pie pieces – pork shoulder
1 onion, peeled and chopped
1 carrot, diced
1 leek, washed and sliced
1 stick celery, chopped
salt and black pepper
450 ml/¾ pint water
1 teaspoon chopped fresh sage
25 g/1 oz sultanas
450 g/1 lb potatoes, peeled and thinly sliced
400 g/14 oz pack frozen puff pastry, or shortcrust pastry made to your preferred recipe
milk or beaten egg, to glaze

Soak the apricots in water to cover for several hours. Preheat the oven to moderate (180°C, 350°F, Gas Mark 4).

Put the pork with the onion, carrot, leek, celery, seasoning and water in an ovenproof casserole and cook in the oven for about 45 minutes.

Strain off and cool the gravy. This part of the recipe is best done the day before as any fat will have time to settle on the gravy and may be easily removed.

Put the pork in a pie dish, sprinkle with the sage, cover with the drained apricots and add the sultanas. Remove the fat from the gravy and moisten the pie with a little gravy. Season to taste.

Cover the pie with a layer of potato slices. Roll out the pastry and use to make a top for the pie. Glaze with a little milk or beaten egg and bake in a preheated hot oven (200°C, 400°F, Gas Mark 6) for 30–40 minutes.

SERVES 4

LEFT Boozy cockled beef (see page 81);
BELOW Bard's special

from BEATRICE CAIRNS
NUTTY STUFFED LAMB

When they were all at home this was a great favourite for the family of BEATRICE CAIRNS, winner of the *Newcastle Evening Chronicle* competition. 'They loved the stuffing and I always had to make extra,' she recalls. 'No one in our house is an expert carver so you can get nice chunks of everything!

'I cooked it one Sunday and put it on the bench to cool. When lunch time arrived the meat was missing. I looked everywhere but it was gone . . . the culprit my Golden Labrador, Sandy. He had never done such a thing before. I didn't laugh at the time but saw the funny side later. I found the string on the lawn!'

1 breast of Northumbrian lamb,
    boned and trimmed (use bones for
    stock or soup)

Stuffing
25 g/1 oz butter
1 onion, peeled and chopped
100 g/4 oz salted peanuts
1 teaspoon dried mixed herbs
75 g/3 oz soft white breadcrumbs
grated rind of 1 orange
1 egg, beaten
freshly ground black pepper

Preheat the oven to moderately hot (190°C, 375°F, Gas Mark 5).

Prepare the meat and set aside. To prepare the stuffing: melt the butter in a pan and gently fry the onion until tender; crunch the peanuts and add along with the herbs, breadcrumbs and orange rind. Bind with beaten egg and season with pepper.

Spread the stuffing along the meat and roll up. Tie securely with string. Bake in the preheated oven for 1½ hours.

Serve the stuffed lamb with boiled carrots, baked onions, roast potatoes and gravy.

Illustrated on page 86.   SERVES 2–3

from JANET ATKIN
BEEF AND STOUT PIE
WITH SUET CRUST

'This recipe has been a favourite in our family for many years,' says JANET ATKIN, Sheffield *Star* competition winner. 'It was handed down from my grandmother, who used to make this tasty meal whenever the family visited. It is a satisfying, family meal – the only problem is being accused of drinking father's stout! It uses readily available ingredients, some of which are produced locally. The Henderson's Relish is made in Sheffield and the stout is brewed in Yorkshire breweries. Start making the pies the day before you intend serving them.'

225 g/8 oz chuck steak, cut into cubes
2 teaspoons plain flour
¼ teaspoon dried mixed herbs
pinch English mustard powder
1 tablespoon oil (corn, sunflower)
1 dessertspoon Henderson's Relish (or
    Worcestershire sauce, if Relish not
    available)
250 ml/8 fl oz sweet stout
120 ml/4 fl oz beef stock or water
salt and pepper
5 or 6 pickling onions peeled and blanched
    in boiling water for 5 minutes
50 g/2 oz button mushrooms, wiped

Suet crust pastry
50 g/2 oz self-raising flour
pinch salt
pinch dried mixed herbs
pinch English mustard powder
25 g/1 oz shredded suet
water, to mix
beaten egg or milk, to glaze

Place the beef cubes, flour, herbs and mustard powder in a plastic bag. Shake well to coat the beef cubes evenly.

Heat half the oil in a flameproof casserole dish. Add the coated beef and cook until brown on all sides. Add the Henderson's Relish, stout and beef stock or water. Bring to the boil slowly, stirring continuously. Add salt and pepper to taste.

Cover and cook gently on top of the stove or in a moderate oven for 2 hours, or until the meat is tender. Remove from heat and leave to go cold – preferably overnight.

The next day, about 1½ hours before you intend serving the pie, make the suet pastry.

Sieve the self-raising flour into a bowl with the salt, herbs and mustard powder. Stir in the beef suet and mix with sufficient water to make a soft dough. Knead until smooth on a lightly floured surface. Leave to stand.

Heat the remaining oil in a frying pan. Add the onions and mushrooms and toss over a moderate heat until lightly browned. Remove from the pan. Skim any fat from the top of the meat mixture and stir in the onions and mushrooms.

Place the mixture in a pie dish, piling the mixture higher than the rim of the dish to prevent the pastry sinking during cooking.

Roll out the suet pastry on a floured surface and cut out a lid to fit the dish. Moisten the rim of the dish with water and place the pastry lid over the filling. Brush with egg or milk and make a slit in the centre. Bake in a pre-heated hot oven (200°C, 400°F, Gas Mark 5) for 45–60 minutes, until the pastry is crisp and golden.

Serve the pie hot with potatoes and fresh vegetables.

MAKES 1 PIE

RIGHT Beef and stout pie with suet crust

from DAISY JARMAN
MARKET DAY HOT POT

DAISY JARMAN, of Sturminster Newton, Dorset, won the *Western Gazette*'s competition with this recipe, handed down to her mother. 'It is useful as it could be left in a slow oven on Market Day and provides a complete hot savoury meal on return. The longer it is left the more savoury it will be,' says Mrs Jarman.

'My mother always made it for us on our weekly trip into the local market town for her 'large shop'. I made it regularly for my family of six and now when my grandchildren stay it is still a favourite when we spend the morning at the Monday Market in Stur. We buy "half a pig" from a local farm and very good it is, too,' Mrs Jarman adds.

750 g/1½ lb potatoes, peeled and sliced
450 g/1 lb onions, peeled and sliced
1 large cooking apple, peeled and diced
6 small pork chops, trimmed
2 pig's kidneys, cored and sliced
1 teaspoon chopped sage (or dried)
salt and black pepper
1 tablespoon tomato sauce
300 ml/½ pint stock

Preheat the oven to cool (150°C, 300°F, Gas Mark 2).

Put a layer of potatoes, onions and apple into a lidded, ovenproof casserole, season, place the chops and kidneys on top, cover with more of the potato, onion and apple mix, seasoning to taste. Finish with a layer of potatoes. Stir the tomato sauce into the stock and pour over the ingredients. Cover and cook in the preheated slow oven for 2–3 hours.

SERVES 6

LEFT Nutty stuffed lamb (see page 84);
BELOW Market day hot pot

from DESIREE MERICAN
HERBED LAMB ROLLS

As a child, DESIREE MERICAN, winner of the *Brighton Evening Argus* competition, spent quite a lot of time at the home of her country grandparents, where this recipe was often used as a mid-week dish and stretched a half shoulder of lamb to serve quite a number of people, Désirée now uses lamb fillets as they are less fatty.

450–750 g/1–1½ lb lamb fillet, very finely minced
2 slices bread (preferably wholemeal), crumbled
1 small onion, peeled and finely chopped
1 teaspoon dried mixed herbs
salt and black pepper

Onion purée
50 g/2 oz butter or margarine
3 large onions, peeled and finely chopped
1 glass dry white wine
1 teaspoon mustard, made up with vinegar (or use French mustard)

Preheat the oven to moderate (180°C, 350°F, Gas Mark 4).

Mix all the ingredients for the lamb rolls together and knead them until they resemble dough. Make into 6–8 sausages, depending on how much meat you started with, and place in a greased oven tin. Bake in the preheated oven for 30 minutes, or until done. Do not overcook or the rolls will become dry.

Meanwhile, make the onion purée. Melt the fat in a saucepan and gently cook the onions until soft but not brown. Add the wine, mustard and salt and pepper to taste. Cover the pan and leave to cook on a low heat until the onions are very soft. Mash them down with a potato masher, or liquidize them. The sauce should not be too dry, so if the onions need more liquid when cooking, add a little hot water.

Serve the rolls and onion purée together.
SERVES 3–4

from MARJORY GARDNER
MINTED PEAR NOISETTES

MARJORY GARDNER was the *Glasgow Evening Times* competition winner with this delicious recipe for lamb chops. She remembers, 'The first time I served this dish one of my guests was still recovering from a throat operation and was unable to eat large pieces of meat. I had hastily to mince his two noisettes and make them into hamburgers, which he thoroughly enjoyed.'

4–8 lamb chops, loin or best end of neck
25 g/1 oz butter
1 medium onion, peeled and chopped
4 large ripe pears, peeled, cored and chopped
2 tablespoons concentrated mint sauce
salt and black pepper
lemon slices, to garnish

Prepare noisettes from the chops by very carefully cutting the meat from the bone (use the bones for stock). Roll the meat into a neat round with the lean part in the centre. Tie into shape with fine string. Cover and put in the refrigerator.

Melt the butter in a frying pan. Add the onion and sauté until soft but not browned. Add the pears and continue cooking for about 5 minutes until the pears are soft. Leave to cool.

When cold, purée the pears and onions in a processor or blender, or push them through a sieve. Add the mint sauce and stir in salt and pepper to taste.

Cover the noisettes with the pear and mint purée, after pricking them on both sides with a fork. Leave for one hour then turn over and leave for another hour.

Drain the noisettes, reserving the purée, and grill under a preheated grill for 2–3 minutes on each side then for 6–8 minutes on a lower heat.

While the chops are grilling, place the purée in a saucepan and cook for 6–8 minutes until it has warmed through.

Remove the noisettes to a warmed serving dish and pour over a little of the pear and mint purée. Garnish with the lemon slices. Serve the remaining pear and mint purée in a sauce boat.
SERVES 4

RIGHT Herbed lamb rolls

from COLIN CULLIMORE
ROAST LEG OF LAMB
with Sherry and Redcurrant Sauce

'Every time I eat roast beef I think it is the best centre for a meal imaginable until British lamb comes into season and then I realise that the moistness and flavour is beyond compare,' says COLIN CULLIMORE, C.B.E., Chairman of the country's largest multiple butchery chain, *J.H. Dewhurst Ltd.* 'Personally, I prefer a saddle because there is the delightful combination of the crisp outside, the succulent slices from the loin and the exquisite tender and pink fillet from underneath.

'Saddle requires a shorter cooking time (15 minutes per 450 g//1 lb) and the oven must be very hot before putting in the joint, then you can turn it down to 180°C, 350°F, Gas Mark 4 after 15 minutes. It is not everyone's choice for carving unless you have a butcher or chef in the family, which is why I have selected a leg for this recipe. If you do have a saddle, remember, always carve the chump end as though it were a leg but the loin *lengthways*.'

1.5–2 kg/3–5 lb leg of lamb
10 small sprigs of fresh rosemary

Sauce
300 ml/½ pint stock
1 tablespoon cornflour
2–3 teaspoons redcurrant jelly
2–3 tablespoons sherry
salt and black pepper

Preheat the oven to hot (220°C, 425°F, Gas Mark 7).

Using a sharp knife, make 10 small incisions in the lamb joint and press a small sprig of rosemary into each cut. Weigh the joint and calculate the cooking time at 20 minutes per 450 g/1 lb. If you prefer lamb well cooked rather than pink, add an extra 20 minutes to the total cooking time.

Place the lamb in a roasting tin and roast in the centre of the preheated oven for 20 minutes. Reduce the heat to moderate (180°C, 350°F, Gas Mark 4) for the remainder of the cooking time.

Remove the lamb from the tin and place it on a serving plate. Drain off any excess fat from the roasting tin, leaving the meat juices in the tin.

As with all roasted meats, leave the joint wrapped in foil or covered with a cloth for at least 10 minutes to allow re-absorption of natural juices.

Meanwhile, in a small bowl, blend 2 tablespoons of the stock with the cornflour, add the rest of the stock to the juices in the roasting tin and mix well together. Bring slowly to the boil, stirring well. Add a little of the hot stock to the blended cornflour, mix well. Add to the pan and bring to the boil, stirring continuously. Boil for 1 minute to thicken.

Add the redcurrant jelly and sherry. Stir well and allow the redcurrant jelly to melt. Season with salt and pepper to taste. Serve the lamb with the sauce, roast potatoes, fresh baby carrots and a few onions baked round the joint.

SERVES 6–8

from CATHY CHAPMAN
BEEF CARBONADE

This version of the classic beef recipe, slightly simpler but just as memorable as the one on page 120, comes from CATHY CHAPMAN, senior food selector for *Marks and Spencer*.

50 g/2 oz butter
50 ml/2 fl oz vegetable oil
450 g/1 lb chuck steak, cubed
25 g/1 oz plain flour
1 tablespoon tomato purée
1 tablespoon wine vinegar
300 ml/½ pint Guinness
salt and black pepper
pinch dried thyme
100 g/4 oz onions, peeled and sliced

Mustard Croûtons
1 tablespoon Dijon mustard
25 g/1 oz butter
slices French bread

Preheat the oven to moderate (160°C, 325°F, Gas Mark 3).

Melt 25 g/1 oz of the butter with 25 ml/1 fl oz of the oil until hot, then seal the meat quickly until all sides are brown. Remove and keep on one side.

Wipe the pan with absorbent kitchen paper, melt the remaining butter, add the flour and cook until golden brown breadcrumbed consistency.

Add the tomato purée and wine vinegar and mix to a smooth paste. Gradually add the Guinness and mix well to ensure a smooth, lump-free sauce. Season to taste with salt, pepper and thyme.

Add the beef. If the sauce does not cover the beef, add and mix sufficient water to ensure the beef is covered. Cook in the preheated oven for $2\frac{1}{2}$ hours.

Heat the remaining oil gently and fry the sliced onions until golden brown. Reserve the onions and juices and add to the casserole after $2\frac{1}{2}$ hours. Cook for another 30 minutes. Adjust the seasoning to taste before serving.

Serve the Carbonade with Mustard croûtons: mix the Dijon Mustard with the butter. Lightly toast one side of sliced French bread. Spread the mustard butter on the plain sides and toast till golden brown. These can be made in advance and reheated in the oven.

SERVES 4   *Beef carbonade*

from JOHN HARDMAN
LAMB NOISETTES WITH KIWI FRUIT SAUCE

JOHN HARDMAN, Chairman of the *ASDA* 'superstore' chain finds this combination of lamb and kiwi fruit irresistible. He suggests it is served accompanied by a selection of fresh vegetables such as green beans, baby sweetcorn and mangetout.

1 kiwi fruit
2.5 cm/1 inch root ginger, peeled and finely chopped
2 garlic cloves, peeled and crushed
2 tablespoons soy sauce
2 tablespoons dry sherry
1 tablespoon brown sugar
grated rind and juice of $\frac{1}{2}$ an orange
1 loin of lamb (approx 1.25–1.5 kg/ $2\frac{1}{2}$–3 lb), boned and rolled

Kiwi fruit sauce
2–3 kiwi fruit, peeled
1 teaspoon lemon juice
1 teaspoon sugar
$\frac{1}{2}$ teaspoon grated orange rind

To garnish
kiwi fruit slices
watercress sprigs

Preheat the oven to moderate (180°C, 350°F, Gas Mark 4).

Peel the kiwi fruit, mash well or liquidize. Place in a bowl and add all the other ingredients, except the lamb. Mix well.

Place the joint of meat in a roasting tin, baste with the marinade, and put in the preheated oven. To cook, allow 20 minutes per 450 g/1 lb, plus 20 minutes. Baste the joint frequently with the marinade.

Meanwhile, make the Kiwi fruit sauce. Mash the kiwi fruit well and add the lemon juice and sugar. (Alternatively, blend the ingredients in an electric mixer.) Mix in the grated orange rind and serve, decorated with thin strips of orange rind, in a bowl.

Remove the cooked meat from the tin and place on a board, reserving the pan juices to make gravy, if you like. Cut the meat into noisettes, making the cuts between the pieces of string. Remove the string.

Place the noisettes on a hot serving plate, cut side uppermost, and garnish with sliced kiwi fruit and watercress. Serve the Kiwi fruit sauce separately.

SERVES 4

Lamb noisettes with kiwi fruit sauce

from ALEC MONK
SPICY PORK CASSEROLE

This delicious casserole of pork is a favourite with ALEC MONK, Chairman and Chief Executive of the *Gateway Corporation plc*.

2 tablespoons vegetable oil
400 g/14 oz cubed pork
1 medium onion, peeled and chopped
100 g/4 oz button mushrooms
1 × 225 g/8 oz can pineapple pieces in natural juice
water, for mixing
4 tablespoons smooth peanut butter
1 tablespoon tomato purée
1 tablespoon brown sugar
1 tablespoon lime juice
1–2 teaspoons chilli powder
2 tablespoons soy sauce
1 green pepper, deseeded and skinned and cut into strips

Preheat the oven to moderate (160°C, 325°F, Gas Mark 3).

Heat 1 tablespoon of the oil in a frying pan, add the meat and fry until evenly browned. Remove the meat from the pan and place in a casserole dish.

Add the onions and mushrooms to the frying pan and cook until soft. Mix with the meat in the casserole.

Drain the juice from the pineapple pieces into a measuring jug and make up to 300 ml/½ pint with water.

Mix the peanut butter, tomato purée, brown sugar, remaining oil, lime juice, chilli powder and soy sauce together in a saucepan. Blend in the juice and water. Heat gently to form a smooth liquid. Pour over the meat in the casserole.

Transfer the casserole to the preheated oven and cook for 1 hour. Add the pineapple pieces and pepper and cook for a further 30 minutes.

The casserole is good served with rice or pasta.

SERVES 4

from SIR DENNIS LANDAU
FRUITY BEEF AND LAMB CASSEROLE

ABOVE Fruity beef and lamb casserole;
LEFT Spicy pork casserole

SIR DENNIS LANDAU, Chief Executive of *CWS*, principal supplier to Britain's retail co-operative societies, likes the mix of meats with fruit in this casserole.

2 tablespoons cooking oil
350 g/12 oz lean stewing beef, cubed
350 g/12 oz lean lamb, cubed
1 large onion, peeled and chopped
1 garlic clove, peeled and crushed
1 green pepper, de-seeded and chopped
¼ teaspoon cayenne pepper
¼ teaspoon mixed spice
salt and black pepper
300 ml/½ pint beef stock or water
50 g/2 oz pre-soaked dried apricots, chopped
1 × 215 g/7½ oz can pitted prunes, drained
25 g/1 oz sultanas
75 g/3 oz canned chickpeas, drained
2 tablespoons apricot jam

Preheat the oven to moderate (180°C, 350°F, Gas Mark 4).

Heat the oil in a large frying pan over a moderate heat. Add the meat cubes, a few at a time, and brown on all sides. Remove the meat with a draining spoon and transfer to a large ovenproof casserole dish.

Sauté the onion, garlic and green pepper in the oil for 5–10 minutes, or until the onion is tender. Using the draining spoon, add the vegetables to the casserole dish and stir in well. Add the stock or water. Transfer the casserole to the pre-heated oven and cook for 1 hour.

Stir in the remaining ingredients, except the jam, and cook for a further 30–60 minutes until the meat is tender. Just before serving, stir in the apricot jam. The casserole may be served on a bed of rice on individual plates.

SERVES 4–6

from DAVID EVANS
ROAST RIB OF BEEF

DAVID EVANS, President of the *National Federation of Meat Traders*, is the fifth generation of his family to have made his living in the congenial surroundings of a traditional butcher's shop in Wales. Although he welcomes the trend to including 'more cosmopolitan' cuts and meats in butchers' shops and, indeed, enjoys all meats, his favourite choice would be Roast Rib of Beef. 'A rib of beef cut from a traditional British breed – Aberdeen Angus, Hereford, Galloway or Welsh Black – well matured, would be hard to beat,' he says.

He suggests choosing a larger piece incorporating several ribs, particularly for a dinner party, since it benefits from the method of cooking he prefers – that is, in a reasonably hot oven, about 180°C, 350°F, Gas Mark 4, 'which results in a joint ready for the carver, beautifully crisp on the outside and succulently moist and tender on the inside.'

The butcher should be asked to chine the joint with his saw along the base of the ribs about 2.5 cm/1 inch above the point at which they join the vertebrae. The vertebrae, including the dorsal processes, can then be removed, together with the 'strap' (the yellow cartilage which runs along the crest), leaving just the individual ribs in the joint.

Cook the meat at the temperature suggested, basting it with its own juices at least once, until it is cooked to your liking.

Mr Evans recently enjoyed just such a joint served with new potatoes (Pembrokes), baby carrots and courgettes fried in butter with a little fresh garlic – no Yorkshire pudding, since there was no room on the plate for that! The gravy was made in the usual manner: the fat was drained off the roasting pan, and some of the water the potatoes were cooked in was added to the meat juices and thickened with a little plain flour.

from ALISTAIR GRANT
SPICY INDIAN ROAST LAMB WITH CABBAGE

This recipe is a favourite with ALISTAIR GRANT, Group Chief Executive of *Argyll Group* plc, which owns the Safeway and Presto superstores.

In the recipe the marinade is finally mixed with the cabbage to become a cross between sauce and vegetable. If you can marinate the lamb overnight, or even for two days, so much the better.

Traditionally, the lamb would have been cooked on an open fire. But a modern oven does a good job, too, especially as the streaks of marinade brown to near blackness, giving a crusty charcoal-grilled effect. If preferred, the cabbage (or any other green vegetable) can be simply boiled rather than baked in the lamb juices, drained and then mixed with the sauce.

half a leg of shank end of lamb, about 1.5 kg/3½ lb
225 g/8 oz Savoy cabbage, shredded finely
4–5 sprigs fresh coriander, chopped coarsely

Marinade
1 garlic clove, peeled and cut into slivers
½ teaspoon ground ginger
½ teaspoon ground cardamom
1 teaspoon paprika
1 heaped teaspoon curry powder or garam masala
2 tablespoons oil
few good twists of the black pepper mill
pinch of salt
150 ml/¼ pint plain unsweetened yogurt

Make slits in the lamb flesh and insert the garlic pieces.

Mix all the remaining marinade ingredients together, and spread over the half-leg. Leave, covered in cling film, in the refrigerator.

Preheat the oven to moderately hot (200°C, 400°F, Gas Mark 6). Lift the lamb out of the marinade (but don't bother to scrape it clean) and lay it in an oiled roasting pan. Roast for 1 hour, basting once or twice with the juices that gather in the pan. Then add the shredded cabbage to the pan, and turn it in the fat and juices. Return to the oven for another 20 minutes. By now the lamb should be barely pink (stick a skewer into the flesh and check the juices – they shouldn't be blood red and the skin should be dark patchy brown).

Lift the lamb out and set aside to rest for 10 minutes while you make the sauce for the cabbage.

With a perforated spoon lift the cabbage out of the pan, and mop up most of the fat on it with absorbent kitchen paper. Pour away the fat in the roasting pan, leaving all but about a tablespoon of juices. Add the rest of the marinade, and stir well, scraping any brown bits off the bottom of the pan. Return the cabbage, mix well and reheat without boiling. (*TIP*: a teaspoon of slaked cornflour helps prevent the yogurt sauce curdling, which it does if boiled. But slightly curdled sauce is most authentic!) Add the coriander and then tip into a serving dish. Serve the cabbage with the lamb and follow with a fresh green salad.
SERVES 4

RIGHT Spicy Indian roast lamb with cabbage

from LORD SAINSBURY
ROAST SADDLE OF LAMB WITH THYME AND MUSTARD SAUCE

LORD SAINSBURY, Chairman of *J. Sainsbury*, greatly enjoys this recipe for lamb, which comes from a Sainsbury's cookery book, *The Josceline Dimbleby Christmas Book*.

juice of 1 lemon
4 tablespoons olive oil, plus extra
2 garlic cloves, peeled and finely chopped
salt and black pepper
a saddle of English lamb
2 tablespoons fresh thyme

Sauce
25 g/1 oz butter
25 g/1 oz cornflour
300 ml/½ pint milk
1 tablespoon fresh thyme
2 teaspoons whole-grain mustard
*2–3 pinches of cayenne pepper or chilli
   powder*
salt

If possible, prepare the joint the night before. Mix the lemon juice in a bowl with the olive oil and chopped garlic and season with salt and black pepper. Rub the lamb all over with this mixture. Sprinkle the thyme on the underside of the meat and press it into any cracks. Leave the joint underside up so that the thyme stays on the flesh. Cover the pan and leave in a cool room for several hours or overnight.

Heat the oven to moderate (180°C, 350°F, Gas Mark 4).

Turn the joint over in the pan and smear the fat with a little more olive oil and salt. Roast in the centre of the preheated oven for 15–25 minutes per 450 g/1 lb, basting occasionally.

When the lamb is nearly ready, start making the sauce. Melt the butter in a saucepan. Remove from the heat and blend in the cornflour. Gradually stir in the milk and bring to the boil, stirring constantly. Simmer gently, still stirring, for 2–3 minutes. Stir in the thyme and mustard.

Remove the lamb from the oven to a carving board and pour away the excess fat from the pan. Add the remaining pan juices to the sauce, then season the sauce to taste with cayenne pepper or chilli powder and salt. Transfer to a sauce boat.

Carve the meat in long, thin strips down the length of the joint and serve with the sauce boat of thyme and mustard sauce.

SERVES 8–12

Roast saddle of lamb with thyme and mustard sauce

from SIR IAN MACLAURIN
FILET DE BOEUF EN CROUTE

This fine version of a classic recipe for beef fillet (more commonly known as Beef Wellington in English) comes from SIR IAN MACLAURIN, Chairman of *Tesco Stores Ltd.*

1.5 kg/3 lb fillet of beef
2 garlic cloves, peeled and sliced (optional)
15 g/½ oz butter
2 tablespoons olive oil
2 tablespoons brandy
salt and black pepper
500 g/1¼ lb frozen puff pastry, thawed
100 g/4 oz pâté de foie gras, at room
   temperature
beaten egg, to glaze

Filet de boeuf en croûte

Preheat the oven to moderately hot (200°C, 400°F, Gas Mark 6).

Trim any fat off the beef and tie it into a neat, regular shape with trussing thread or string. With a sharp pointed knife, make shallow incisions all over the meat at regular intervals. Insert the garlic slices into the incisions.

Melt the butter with the oil in a flameproof casserole or large, heavy-based frying pan. Add the meat and fry over a moderate heat until well browned and sealed on all sides. Roast in the oven for 15 minutes.

Warm the brandy in a clean small pan. Remove the meat in its pan from the oven, pour the brandy over and ignite. When the flames have died down, lift the meat out of the roasting pan and set aside until cold. Reserve the juices in the pan.

Roll out the pastry to a size that will wrap

round the meat. Gently spread out the pâté on the centre of the pastry and place the cooled meat on it. Wrap the pastry around the meat, sealing the joints with water.

Place the pastry-wrapped meat, join side down, on a dampened baking sheet. Decorate with any left-over pastry trimmings, sticking them on with water. Brush with beaten egg.

Bake in the oven (200°C, 400°F, Gas Mark 6) for 55–60 minutes, according to how well done you like your beef.

At the end of the cooking time, turn off the oven and leave the meat to 'rest' for 15 minutes before serving.

Meanwhile, make a gravy from the meat juices left over in the pan. Add 90 ml/6 tablespoons Madeira, port or dry sherry, if desired. Transfer the fillet to a serving plate and carve at the table.

SERVES 6

from MARK BUTLER
MIGNONETTE OF LAMB WITH SPINACH AND MUSHROOMS

This delicate combination of lamb and vegetables is one of the repertoire of recipes served by the caterer, *Ring and Brymer*, caterers at such prestigious events as the Chelsea Flower Show, Cartier International Polo and the Hennessy Gold Cup. The company's managing director, MARK BUTLER, enjoys it, and emphasises that the lamb fillet must be very carefully trimmed, leaving no trace of fat or sinew.

450 g/1 lb lamb bones
100 g/4 oz carrots, chopped
50 g/2 oz leeks, chopped
1 onion, peeled and chopped
1 garlic clove, peeled
1 bouquet garni
2 lamb fillets, approx. 225 g/8 oz each
butter, for frying
3 shallots, peeled and chopped
150 ml/¼ pint white wine
150 ml/¼ pint olive oil
350 g/12 oz mushrooms, washed and finely chopped
1 small bunch fresh basil
450 g/1 lb leaf spinach
salt and black pepper

Spread out the lamb bones in a buttered roasting tray and brown in a moderately hot oven (190°C, 375°F, Gas Mark 5).

Place the browned bones, carrots, leeks, onion, garlic and bouquet garni in a large pot with 3.5 litres/6 pints of water, and simmer for 3 hours, skimming at intervals.

Remove all the bones with a slotted spoon, reduce the liquid to 600 ml/1 pint, and liquidize. Set the stock aside.

Season the two pieces of lamb with salt and pepper. Fry them in butter for 4 minutes on each side until they are still pink inside. Set aside.

Take the pan that has been used to cook the lamb in and add two chopped shallots and some more butter. Let the shallots soften, then add the white wine. Reduce by half, then add the lamb stock and liquidized vegetables. Strain the sauce, season to taste and correct the consistency, if necessary.

Heat the olive oil in a pan, add the mushrooms and sauté. Drain, and sauté again with the remaining shallot and basil. Drain once more. Set aside.

Remove the stalks from the spinach and wash it carefully. Cook the spinach in a little boiling salted water for 10 seconds. Drain, refresh in cold running water and drain well again.

Now preheat the oven to moderate (160°C, 325°F, Gas Mark 3).

To assemble the mignonettes, you will need 4 metal rings approximately 10 cm/4 inches in diameter and 2 cm/¾ inch deep, or pieces of stiff card stapled together at the ends and wrapped in tin foil.

Place each ring in the middle of an ovenproof serving plate. Fill each ring with successive layers of spinach and mushrooms, pressing each layer down as you go. Each ring should be about three-quarters full. Warm in a pre-heated oven.

Carve the lamb into very thin slices and arrange the slices around the top of each ring, as if you were making an apple tart. Reheat for 30 seconds in a hot oven. Carefully remove the metal rings or cards to reveal the layers of spinach and mushroom underneath the lamb, and serve, surrounded by the sauce.

SERVES 4

from NEVILLE WATSON
FILLET OF BEEF RUMFORD

This delicious recipe was devised by the private catering company, *Beeton Rumford* and was contributed by the company's Managing Director, NEVILLE WATSON. It has proved to be a popular dish at the many very special parties they cater for at places like London's South Bank Concert Halls and Europe's two largest independent exhibition centres, Earls Court and Olympia.

Allow 2 days to make this dish, since the meat is best marinated overnight. The stuffing should also be made the day before it is required.

2.25 kg/5 lb fillet of beef

Marinade
½ head celery, washed and roughly chopped
225 g/8 oz carrots, scrubbed and chopped
225 g/8 oz onions, peeled and chopped
salt
black peppercorns
4 bay leaves
½ bottle red wine
1.2 litres/2 pints oil

Stuffing
1 kg/2 lb button mushrooms, wiped clean
25 g/1 oz butter
75 g/3 oz shallots, peeled and finely
*   chopped*
1 bay leaf
salt and black pepper
275 g/10 oz chicken pâté

To cook the fillet
1 kg/2 lb back bacon, rinded
100 g/4 oz onions, peeled and chopped
100 g/4 oz carrots, peeled and chopped
50 g/2 oz celery, washed and chopped
120 ml/4 fl oz oil

Trim the beef fillet, remove the chine and all the silver skin.

For the marinade, place the chopped vegetables in a container deep enough for the wine and oil to half cover the fillet. Add the salt and peppercorns and bay leaves. Pour in the wine and oil and mix together.

Put the fillet in the marinade, ensuring it is well mixed. Cover with greaseproof paper. Refrigerate for 6–8 hours, turning the fillet every 2 hours, or overnight.

Meanwhile, make the stuffing. Finely chop the button mushrooms.

Melt the butter in a small pan, add the shallots and cook until transparent, then add the button mushrooms, bay leaf and seasoning. Cook over a medium heat for a few minutes, then turn up the heat to reduce the liquid.

When the vegetables are cooked, strain off and discard any liquid and leave to cool. When cold, mix well with the chicken pâté and leave in the refrigerator overnight.

The next day, remove the fillet from the marinade, making sure no vegetables are left on it. Season with salt and pepper.

Put 3–4 tablespoons of clean oil in a pan and heat. When it is very hot, carefully put the fillet in the pan and brown all over very quickly, to seal in the juices. Remove the fillet from the pan and set aside to cool.

Tunnel down the fillet from the thick end until about 10 cm/4 inches from the tail end. Tuck under the tail end. Pipe in the mushroom and pâté mixture, making sure it goes down the whole fillet.

Now preheat the oven to moderate (180°C, 350°F, Gas Mark 4).

Lay out two bacon rashers, thin end to thin end, then two more slightly overlapping, continuing until the bacon 'wrap' is the length of the fillet. Lay the fillet on top of the bacon and wrap the bacon round the fillet, making sure the fillet is well covered. Tie with string to hold the bacon in place.

Place the chopped vegetables in a roasting pan with a little of the oil. Lay the fillet on top, brushing the remainder of the oil over it. Cook in the oven for 1 hour.

SERVES 10

Fillet of beef Rumford

from ALAN PAYNE
LAMB CUTLETS WITH ESPAGNOLE SAUCE

Payne and Gunter, the long-established catering company whose clients include the Open Championship Golf, Henley Royal Regatta and Goodwood racecourse, have been looking back in their archives to the days when Gunters, established in the 18th century, served meals to royalty, including British kings and French emperors, adapting many old recipes for use today. This recipe, provided by ALAN PAYNE, the company's Managing Director, is based on one much appreciated by King William IV. Espagnole sauce is so-called because Spanish ham was originally used to make it, instead of bacon.

Stock
900 g/2 lb shin of beef with bone
butter or fat for frying
2 litres/4 pints water
2 carrots, sliced
2 onions, peeled and sliced
1 bouquet garni
2 bay leaves
½ tablespoon black peppercorns
salt

Espagnole sauce
50 g/2 oz butter
50 g/2 oz bacon, diced
1 carrot, sliced
1 onion, peeled and sliced
1 bouquet garni
1 bay leaf
1 clove
4 peppercorns
40 g/1½ oz cornflour
1 litre/2 pints strong brown stock
75 g/3 fl oz dry sherry
3 tablespoons tomato purée
salt and black pepper

8 lamb cutlets
2 eggs, beaten
dried breadcrumbs

For the stock, remove the meat from the bones and cube it, removing all the skin and fat. Brown the meat in the fat or butter. Transfer to a large saucepan, using a slotted spoon so that as much fat as possible is left behind. Add the bones, and the remaining stock ingredients to the saucepan. Bring to the boil and simmer gently for about 4 hours, skimming off the scum from time to time. Strain and leave to cool. When the stock is cold remove every trace of fat. This will make about 1 litre (2 pints) of strong stock.

For the Espagnole sauce, melt the butter in a heavy saucepan. Add the chopped bacon and vegetables and fry gently until golden. Add the herbs, clove and peppercorns. Stir into the butter and allow to sweat gently for 5 minutes. Add the cornflour and brown gently, adding a little more butter if necessary. Remove the pan from the heat and add stock, sherry and tomato purée. Return to the heat, bring to the boil and simmer gently for 1½ hours. Strain the sauce and leave to cool. Skim off any fat, reheat and season before serving.

To prepare the lamb cutlets, scrape the last 1.5 cm/¾ inch of each cutlet bone bare of meat. Beat the cutlets a little to flatten them, so they are more or less a uniform shape. Dip the cutlets into the beaten egg and breadcrumbs, pressing the crumbs firmly on to the meat with a knife. Repeat if necessary to give a good coating. Grill under a very hot, preheated grill for about 2–3 minutes on either side. Place a paper frill on the end of each cutlet. Arrange on a heated, flat dish surrounded by piped mashed potato. Serve with the Espagnole sauce and peas.

If you like your cutlets very well cooked, omit the egg and breadcrumbs which will char if over-cooked. Brush the cutlets with melted butter instead.

SERVES 4

from FRED SHASKO
PORK A LA CREME GROSVENOR

This recipe was devised by FRED SHASKO, chef with the catering company, *Compass*. The company includes amongst its clients Harrods, the Britannia Royal Naval College at Dartmouth, Austin Rover, The Scottish Exhibition Centre and Sheffield Wednesday Football Club. The pork 'griskins' in Mr Shasko's recipe are the pieces left by the butcher when he trims pork fillet; if they are not available, use pork fillet itself.

100 g/4 oz margarine
1 medium onion, peeled and finely diced
750 g/1½ lb trimmed and sliced (approx. 5 mm/¼ inch slices) pork griskins
salt and black pepper
3 garlic cloves, peeled and crushed
50 g/2 oz white wine (sweet or dry)
100 g/4 oz plain flour
600 ml/1 pint hot chicken stock
pinch of tarragon (dried)
4–5 bay leaves (dried)
100 g/4 oz mushrooms, finely sliced
1 green pepper, finely diced
300 ml/½ pint single cream

Melt the margarine in a 2.25 litre/4 pint saucepan over a medium heat. Add the onion and sauté until the colour changes, but they are not browned. Add the pork, salt, pepper, garlic and wine. Cook gently for a few minutes until the meat is sealed.

Add the flour and stir with a wooden spoon until the liquid is absorbed. Cook for 2 minutes. Add the hot chicken stock slowly, stirring continuously, until a thick sauce is formed. Add the tarragon, bay leaves, mushrooms and pepper. Simmer for 1 hour, stirring all the time.

Remove the bay leaves and add the cream just before serving. If the sauce becomes too thick during cooking, add a little more stock.

SERVES 4
RIGHT Pork a la crème Grosvenor

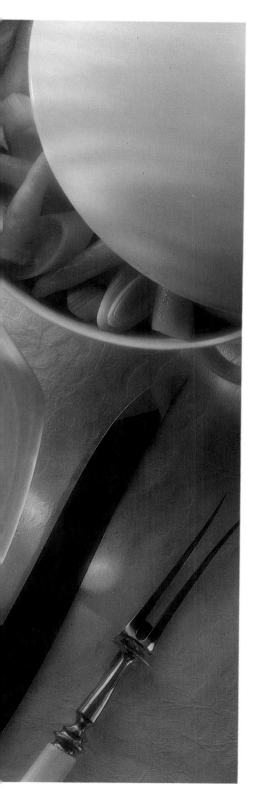

from ROBERT KELSO
LOIN OF VEAL STUFFED WITH APRICOTS AND PISTACHIOS

ROBERT KELSO, Managing Director of *Leith's Good Food (Party Catering)*, finds that this recipe for veal is always much appreciated. Leith's Good Food, begun by Prue Leith in 1961, are responsible for the catering at London's newest and largest conference centre, the Queen Elizabeth II Centre, and are the appointed caterers to the Orient Express.

1 large onion, peeled and sliced
3 chicken breasts, skinned
425 g/15 oz dried apricots, sliced
1 tablespoon finely chopped tarragon
1 tablespoon finely chopped parsley
50 g/2 oz pistachios
salt
freshly ground black pepper
2 kg/4½ lb boned loin of veal
600 ml/1 pint veal stock or wine

Preheat the oven to moderately hot (200°C, 400°F, Gas Mark 6).

Using a food processor, purée the onion, add the chicken breasts and continue blending at high speed until they reach a smooth, even consistency.

Place in a bowl, add the apricots, herbs, pistachios and seasoning. Mix well. Lay the meat out flat, skin side down, and place the stuffing on the meat. Roll up and secure with string.

Roast in a preheated oven in a shallow roasting tin with the stock/wine poured around, for 20 minutes per 450 g/1 lb, plus 20 minutes. Baste the meat frequently during cooking.

SERVES 10

Loin of veal stuffed with apricots and pistachios

from LORD FORTE
FAUX FILET DE BOEUF AU POIVRE ROSE
(Roast sirloin of beef with pink peppercorns)

LORD FORTE, Chairman of *Trust House Forte* plc, the international hotel, catering and leisure group likes this splendid and stylish recipe for roast beef.

3.5 kg/8 lb trimmed sirloin of beef
120 ml/4 fl oz oil
salt and pepper
25 g/1 oz shallots, peeled and finely chopped
275 g/10 oz pink peppercorns
50 g/2 oz butter
175 ml/6 fl oz red wine
175 ml/6 fl oz jus lie

Preheat the oven to hot (220°C, 425°F, Gas Mark 7).

Place the sirloin of beef in a roasting tray. Add the oil and seasonings. On top of the stove seal the beef, then transfer it to a preheated oven. Cook the beef to your liking.

Remove the beef from the pan and pour off the fat. Add the shallots, peppercorns and 1 oz butter to the roasting pan and stir. Add the wine, pour in the jus lie and stir well.

Transfer to a saucepan, bring to the boil and reduce to the required consistency. Season to taste and stir in the remainder of the butter. Pass through a fine chinois (strainer) into a warmed sauce boat.

Carve the beef, arrange on a warmed serving dish and pour the sauce around.

SERVES 16–20

from PETER HOWELL
ORIENTAL BEEF STIR-FRY

PETER HOWELL, Managing Director of Specialist Services for *Gardner Merchant*, the major catering group with Europe-wide interests in catering management, consultancy and vending services for industry, commerce, hospitals and schools, likes this recipe for its oriental overtones and the fact that it is ideal for preparing and serving to large numbers.

2½ tablespoons cornflour
8 tablespoons soy sauce
2½ teaspoons caster sugar
salt and black pepper
1.25 kg/2½ lb lean rump steak, cut in strips
5 tablespoons oil
225 g/8 oz button mushrooms, sliced
1 red pepper, seeded, cored and sliced
1 green pepper, seeded, cored and sliced
275 g/10 oz bean sprouts
150 g/5 oz palm hearts, sliced
rind and juice of 2 oranges
450 ml/¾ pint beef stock

Mix together the cornflour, soy sauce, sugar, salt and pepper to make a marinade. Cut the steak into strips, add it to the marinade, cover and leave overnight. Next day, remove the steak from the marinade and drain.

Heat 2½ tablespoons of the oil in a wok or frying pan and cook the mushrooms and peppers for 4 minutes. Drain and place on one side. Stir-fry the beef in the remaining oil for approx. 4 minutes. Add the mushrooms and peppers and stock, cover the pan and cook for 7 minutes.

Just before the stir-fry is ready to serve, add the bean sprouts, sliced palm hearts, orange rind and juice. Cook, stirring gently, for 3 minutes.

Turn the stir-fry into a heated serving dish and serve with plain boiled rice.

SERVES 10

RIGHT Oriental beef stir-fry;
FAR RIGHT Blanquette d'agneau Elizabeth

from LADY ELIZABETH ANSON
BLANQUETTE D'AGNEAU ELIZABETH
(Blanquette of lamb with a saffron sauce)

This recipe, contributed by LADY ELIZABETH ANSON, founder of *Party Planners* who cater for many of the country's top society events, was concocted by Lady Elizabeth and Anton Mosimann, former head chef at the Dorchester Hotel, London, to be one of the dishes available at Mr Mosimann's new club, which opened in London in 1988.

750 g/1¾ lb lamb (breast and shoulder),
    trimmed of all fat
600 ml/1 pint lamb stock, well seasoned
100 ml/4 fl oz white wine
150 g/5 oz bouquet garni (onions, carrots,
    celery, ¼ bay leaf, clove, mint, some
    parsley stalks)
some saffron strands
2 egg yolks
150 ml/¼ pint whipping cream
10 ml/½ fl oz lemon juice
salt and pepper

To garnish
30 g / 1¼ oz glazed baby onions (see below)
50 g / 2 oz carrots, turned (see Note below)
50 g / 2 oz turnips, turned (see Note below)
50 g / 2 oz fine green beans

Cut the lamb into pieces weighing 40 g (1½ oz) each. Blanch in salted water, cool and rinse. Place the meat in a suitable-size, heavy based pan, add the lamb stock and white wine. Bring to the boil and skim. Add the bouquet garni and saffron strands and simmer until the meat is tender, occasionally skimming off the fat.

Meanwhile, prepare the baby onions. First blanch them in boiling water to remove the skins. Cook the skinned onions slowly in a heavy covered pan in a little butter, stock and sugar, until the stock has reduced and the onion are sticky, shining and tender.

Remove the cooked meat from the pan and keep warm. Strain the stock through a fine sieve and reduce it by half.

Meanwhile, cook the other garnish vegetables in salted water until crisp.

Mix the egg yolks with the cream and add to the stock. *The sauce must not be boiled after adding the egg yolks.* Strain the liaised sauce through a fine muslin, then add the lemon juice and season with salt and pepper.

Arrange the meat on a serving dish and cover with the sauce. Garnish with the carrots, turnips and green beans and the freshly glazed baby onions.

SERVES 4

NOTE: 'Turned' vegetables are ones which have been neatly trimmed into even-sized oblongs then pared down into a smooth-surface elongated barrel shape.

from EDWARD DENNY
ROAST SIRLOIN OF ENGLISH BEEF

This superb recipe for beef comes from EDWARD DENNY, Chef Director at the long-established and stylish *The Box Tree* restaurant, Ilkley, West Yorkshire.

*1 × 900 g/2 lb piece of sirloin of beef, off
   the bone but left whole
salt and black pepper
450 ml/¾ pint red wine
4 large shallots, peeled and chopped
1 punnet blueberries (about 225 g/8 oz)
900 ml/1½ pints veal stock
50 g/2 oz butter
6 large sprigs chervil*

Preheat the oven to very hot (240°C, 475°F, Gas Mark 9).

Season the beef well and open roast in the very hot oven for 10 minutes. Remove from the oven, turn over and allow to rest.

Over a fierce heat, reduce the red wine, with the chopped shallots and half the blueberries, to a thick syrup. Then add the veal stock and reduce by two-thirds. Season to taste and pass through a fine sieve.

Return the sauce to a high heat and bring to the boil. Reduce the heat a little and whisk in the butter. (Do not reboil.)

Add the remaining blueberries to the sauce and allow to warm through.

Place the sirloin of beef in a very hot oven for 3 minutes or so to heat through. Rest for 15 minutes. To serve, coat the sirloin with a little sauce and garnish with chervil.

SERVES 6

from ANTON EDELMANN
TOURNEDOS BACCHUS

This elegant recipe is one which ANTON EDELMANN, *Maître Chef des Cuisines* at the *Savoy*, London, prepares for diners there. It is an expensive recipe for the home cook and the initial preparation, especially for the Sauce Vin Rouge, a classic French sauce, is time-consuming, but the result is more than worth the effort. (Recipes for the sauce may be found in such standard reference books as *Larousse Gastronomique*; alternatively, red wine is an acceptable substitute.)

*25 g/1 oz shallots, peeled and chopped
   finely
100 g/4 oz wild mushrooms
100 g/4 oz prepared snails, sliced
25 g/1 oz chopped chives
salt and black pepper
200 g/7 oz tournedos of beef (or 4
   tournedos)
4 Pommes Savoyard (see recipe below)
25 g/1 oz butter
100 ml/3½ fl oz Sauce Vin Rouge*

Sweat the shallots in a pan, add the wild mushrooms and continue to sweat. Add the sliced snails and chives and season well.

In a separate pan, cook the tournedos in a little butter and fat until rare.

Sit each tournedos half on a Pomme Savoyard. Monte au beurre the Sauce vin rouge (that is, melt the butter on top of the warmed sauce) and pour over the tournedos, but not over the Savoyard.

Place some of the mushroom and snail garnish on top of each tournedos and on top of the sauce.

Serve immediately.

POMMES SAVOYARD

*50 g/2 oz butter
50 ml/2 fl oz oil
400 g/14 oz potatoes, cut into small
   cylinders
20 g/¾ oz truffle
salt and black pepper*

Slice the potatoes to approximately 2–3 mm/⅛ inch thick. Dry and toss very quickly in the hot oil.

Season and arrange neatly in 4 small round non-stick moulds. Put in one layer of potato and one layer of truffle – to be approximately only 1 cm/½ inch high.

Brown on a very hot stove, then bake in a hot oven (200°C, 400°F, Gas Mark 6) for approximately 20 minutes, until cooked.

SERVES 4

RIGHT Tournedos Bacchus

from DAVID ADLARD
ROSETTE OF ENGLISH LAMB
with meaux mustard and rosemary, with a 'gâteau' of aubergine and tomato coulis

DAVID ADLARD'S recipe for lamb may be found on the menu at *Adlard's*, his exciting new restaurant in Norwich, Norfolk, where he is both chef and patron.

1 pair of best end of neck of lamb
300 ml/½ pint reduced brown lamb stock
* (see below)*
1 shallot, peeled and diced
1 garlic clove, peeled and diced
40 rosemary spikes (approx.), chopped
1 aubergine
salt and black pepper
oil for frying
300 ml/½ pint thick tomato coulis
1 × 150 ml/¼ pint pot plain yogurt
150 ml/¼ pint Malmsey madeira
arrowroot
Meaux mustard
50 g/2 oz unsalted butter
white breadcrumbs
50 g/2 oz melted butter

Chine out the rack of lamb, trim off the excess fat and cut the bones above the nut of meat (or ask the butcher to do this, making sure he gives you the bones). You will have four fillets.

Use the bones and the trimmings, ideally simmered in a veal stock base, to make lamb stock.

Sweat the shallot and garlic in a little oil or butter for 3 minutes. Add the rosemary and sweat for 1 more minute.

Cut the aubergine in circles 2 mm/1/16 inch thick, lay the circles on a tray lined with absorbent kitchen paper and sprinkle lightly with salt. After 45 minutes pat the slices with paper to absorb the bitter juice, then fry them quickly in a pan containing 1 cm/½ inch oil, but do not allow them to brown. Drain on absorbent kitchen paper.

Line 4 ramekins with the aubergines. Fill each ramekin half full with tomato coulis

and add a quarter of the yoghurt to each. Top up with the tomato and fold over the aubergine. Cover with foil and set aside.

Preheat the oven to moderately hot (200°C, 400°F, Gas Mark 6).

Put the madeira in a saucepan and reduce to a third. Add the lamb stock and reduce, skimming from time to time, to obtain about 300 ml/½ pint, or a little less.

When the reduction has a good strong taste add a little arrowroot to thicken the sauce slightly. Add some Meaux mustard to taste, season and whisk in the unsalted butter. Keep the sauce hot.

Season the lamb and brown in a flameproof casserole on top of the stove. Transfer to the preheated oven and cook for 10–15 minutes. Rest for 10 minutes.

Cut the meat away from the remaining bones and trim off any excess fat. Cover the fat rounded area of the meat with the shallot/rosemary mixture and cover with breadcrumbs. Moisten the breadcrumbs with melted butter and brown under the grill.

Warm the aubergine ramekins in the oven. Turn out on absorbent kitchen paper to drain away excess oil. Cut up the lamb in neat rounds, making 4–5 per person. Pour the sauce carefully on to individual plates and arrange the meat and an aubergine 'gâteau' on each one.

SERVES 4

LEFT Rosette of English lamb with meaux mustard and rosemary and a 'gâteau' of aubergine and tomato coulis

from CAROL TREVOR-ROPER
PORK FILLETS AND SHREDDED PINK LEEKS WITH A PORT SAUCE

Leeks pink with grenadine add delicate colour to this recipe from CAROL TREVOR-ROPER, owner and chef at *Brookdale House*, a secluded Victorian gothic restaurant at North Huish, in Devon.

2 pork fillets, trimmed
4 rashers of smoked bacon, trimmed
8 leeks
50 g/2 oz unsalted butter
3 tablespoons Grenadine
salt and black pepper

Sauce
175 ml/6 fl oz red wine
450 ml/¾ pint brown veal stock
75 ml/3 fl oz port
1 bay leaf
1 sprig of thyme

Preheat the oven to hot (230°C, 450°F, Gas Mark 8).

Place the bacon lengthways either side of the fillets (2 rashers per fillet). Wrap each fillet tightly in foil and cook in the oven for 25–30 minutes, until cooked through. Remove from the oven and keep warm.

Trim, wash and shred the leeks finely. Melt the butter in a pan and soften the leeks for 5 minutes until lightly browned. add the Grenadine and cook for a further 5 minutes. Season with salt and pepper and remove the leeks with a slotted spoon. Keep warm.

For the sauce, pour the wine into the pan and reduce to two tablespoons. Add the stock, port, bay leaf and thyme and reduce by a quarter. Pass through a sieve. Carefully unroll the pork fillets and pour the juices into the sauce. Reduce the sauce again to a slightly syrupy consistency.

Discard the bacon and slice the fillets. Place the leeks on 4 warmed plates, arrange slices of pork around the leeks and spoon the sauce over.
Illustrated on page 2   SERVES 4

from RAYMOND BLANC
CÔTE DE VEAU RÔTIE AUX MOUSSERONS

(Roast veal cutlet served with its own juices spiked with wild mushrooms)

This dish comes from RAYMOND BLANC, chef and owner of the Michelin three star-rated restaurant, *Le Manoir aux Quat' Saisons* in Great Milton, Oxfordshire. The recipe first appeared in M. Blanc's book, *Le Manoir aux Quat' Saisons*, published in February 1988.

Côte de veau rôtie aux mousserons

4 × 350 g/12 oz veal cutlets, trimmed weight
salt and freshly ground white pepper
2 teaspoons unsalted butter
2 teaspoons groundnut oil

Sauce
300 ml/½ pint water
150 g/5 oz fresh mousserons or 20 g/¾ oz dried
20 g/¾ oz unsalted butter
a squeeze of lemon

Preheat the oven to hot (230°C, 450°F, Gas Mark 8).

First remove all pieces of vegetation stuck to the mushrooms then cut off the stalk right under the cap. (The stalks are woody and inedible; dry them and keep for flavouring sauces.) Wash the mushrooms briefly in plenty of cold water, drain and wrap in a tea towel.

Season the cutlets with salt and pepper. Heat the butter and groundnut oil in a roasting pan until hot, then brown the cutlets for 2 minutes per side. Roast in the preheated oven for about 15 minutes, turning them over after 7 minutes. Stand the cutlets upright in another dish so that they do not soak in the juices they will release,

and leave in a warm place. Spoon off most of the fat in the roasting pan.

Place the roasting pan over a medium heat and add 300 ml/½ pint cold water, scraping up all the tasty caramelized juices in the bottom of the pan. Strain into a small saucepan, bring to the boil, skim off any remaining fat and reduce to about 100 ml/4 fl oz juices. Taste and correct seasoning with a pinch of salt and pepper. Set aside.

In a small saucepan, bring to the boil 3 tablespoons cold water and 20 g/¾ oz butter, with a large pinch of salt and 4 turns of pepper. Add the mushrooms, cover and cook for 1 minute; add them to the juices.

Return the veal cutlets to the oven for 5 minutes, seasoning each with a few grains of salt. Strain the juices released by the cutlets into the sauce, taste and correct the seasoning with a little salt and pepper. Lift the juices with a squeeze of lemon.

Place each veal cutlet in the centre of a warm plate and spoon the sauce and mushrooms over and around.

SERVES 4

from KEITH STANLEY
PORK AND PRUNE HOTCH-POTCH

KEITH STANLEY, Head Chef at the *Ritz* in London, says of this dish that it is simple to prepare in a short time, and looks very pleasant in its presentation.

6 × 50 g/2 oz pork fillets
175 g/6 oz potatoes, steamed and grated
75 g/3 oz apples, grated
15 g/½ oz chopped parsley
salt and black pepper
25 g/1 oz oil and butter, mixed, for cooking
50 g/2 oz prunes, liquidized
50 g/2 oz minced pork trimmings
chicken stock, for poaching
25 ml/1 fl oz Kummel
50 ml/2 fl oz double cream
120 ml/4 fl oz jus lie

Cut the pork into uniform pieces, keeping them as round as possible. Mix the potatoes with the apple and seasonings and fry in two 'cakes' in a little oil and butter in a small omelette pan until golden. Mix the prunes with the pork trimmings (from the tails of the fillets) and blend well to achieve a smooth texture. Shape into dumplings with a small spoon and poach in a little chicken stock. Season the pork and pan fry in hot oil

and butter. When the pork is *just* cooked, take it out of the pan and keep warm. Swill the pan with the Kummel and add the cream and jus lie. Bring to the boil and correct the seasoning, if necessary.

To serve, press the fillets of pork on to the potato cakes, sprinkle with prune dumplings, and pour the sauce around.

SERVES 2

BELOW Pork and prune hotch-potch

from MARJAN LESNIK
COCHON DE LAIT FARCI SARLADAISE
(Roast stuffed suckling pig sarladaise)

MARJAN LESNIK, *Maître Chef des Cuisines* at *Claridge's* in London, takes the difficulty out of cooking a suckling pig with this splendid, easy-to-follow recipe.

1 suckling pig

Stuffing
1.5 kg/3 lb onions
450 g/1 lb breadcrumbs
50 g/2 oz sage
50 g/2 oz thyme
2 bay leaves
25 g/1 oz rosemary
225 g/8 oz sausage meat
2 eggs
salt and black pepper
pinch nutmeg

Make sure the suckling pig is correctly trimmed and prepared by the butcher.

To prepare the stuffing, first bake the onions in their skin in a hot oven for about 45 minutes, then peel and chop them finely.

Put the onion in a bowl with the other stuffing ingredients and mix together thoroughly.

Preheat the oven to moderately hot (190°–200°C, 375°–400°F, Gas Mark 5–6).

Use the stuffing to fill the belly of the suckling pig, leaving a little room for the stuffing to expand as it cooks. Sew up the full length of the belly to seal it completely.

Place the suckling pig in a large roasting tray in the preheated oven and cook for approximately 2 hours 15 minutes, basting the suckling pig frequently with oil. By this time the meat should be cooked: the essential point is that the pig should be just done when the skin is crisp and golden.

Increase the oven temperature to hot (230°C, 450°F, Gas Mark 8) and continue cooking the suckling pig for 10–15 minutes to achieve a crisp, golden crackling.

Serve the suckling pig on a silver tray, with apple sauce, gravy and sarladaise potatoes cooked in the fat from the suckling pig (see recipe below).

NOTE: The suckling pig may be spit-roasted. M. Lesnik recommends that a spit-roasted suckling pig should be basted with beer (an ordinary lager is fine) during cooking, a method which also works well with an oven-roasted suckling pig.

GARNITURE: MATEFAIM DE POMMES DE TERRE

800 g–1 kg/1½–2 lb medium-size potatoes
200 ml/⅓ pint pork fat from suckling pig
salt and black pepper
6 round medallions of truffles
10 g/¼ oz chopped truffles

Wash, peel and slice thinly on a mandolin three-quarters of the potatoes.

Take the remaining potatoes and turn half of them into cylinder shapes and slice into thin discs. Cut the rest of the potatoes into thin slices in rectangular shapes, about 2.5 cm/1 inch × 6 cm/2½ inch.

Heat some of the pork fat in an Anna mould (a straight-sided, covered dish, about 18–20 cm/7–8 inch in diameter) until it is very hot. Then line the bottom of the mould with the discs of potato, overlapping them to achieve a rosette effect.

Place one of the truffle medallions in the centre of the potatoes in the dish and the other five round the edge. Line the sides of the mould with the rectangles of potato.

Quickly toss the rest of the potatoes in the remaining pork fat, season them, then lay them in the mould in layers, sprinkling each layer with a little of the chopped truffles, until the mould is full. Press the layers down, seal the top and cook in a hot oven (220°C, 425°F, Gas Mark 7) for 35 minutes.

Drain off any excess fat and turn the potato 'cake' out of the mould.

from MARK SALTER
LOIN OF JACOB LAMB
stuffed with apricots, basil and garlic, served with a charlotte of aubergine, glazed schupfnudeln and tarragon sauce

MARK SALTER, Chef at the quietly elegant and very imposing *Cromlix House*, Kinbuck, Dunblane, in Perthshire, has devised this recipe for Jacob lamb. The Jacob sheep is an ancient breed. Some say that the Biblical Jacob's coat of many colours came from it. Its flesh is a deep red colour, but its flavour is distinctly lamb. Other lamb may be used in this recipe if the Jacob lamb is not available.

1 loin of Jacob lamb
3 large onions, peeled
2 large carrots, scrubbed
3 garlic cloves, peeled and sliced
2 teaspoons finely chopped celeriac
1 tablespoon tomato purée
2 teaspoons sugar
8 litres/14 pints good chicken or beef stock (chicken, for preference, because of its neutral flavour)

Jus seasoning for stock
½ bay leaf
sprig thyme
2 teaspoons sliced green of leek
2 teaspoons crushed white peppercorn

Stuffing (veal farce)
200 g/7 oz lean veal
salt and pepper
1 egg white
100 g/4 oz chilled double cream
50 g/2 oz finely diced apricot
¼ garlic clove, peeled and chopped
1 teaspoon finely sliced basil
100 g/4 oz crepinette (cawl fat)
1 large leek, washed and trimmed

To garnish
1 teaspoon finely chopped fresh tarragon
100 g/4 oz mangetout
50 g/2 oz tomato, finely diced

Bone out the loin of lamb so that you are left with the loin fillet and brown the bones and trimmings in a hot oven. Add a small mirepoix of vegetables (i.e. a mixture of diced or chopped vegetables used as a flavour enhancer) halfway through roasting.

Cut the onions and carrots into mirepoix (dice) and brown in a highsided saucepan. Add the garlic and celeriac and stir in well. Mix in the tomato purée and déglacé (i.e. dilute) with water three times to obtain the colour needed. Fill up with the chicken stock and add the well drained lamb bones. After 3 hours of cooking add the jus seasoning ingredients.

For the stuffing, cut the veal into fine strips. Season well and add the egg white. Pass through the finest blade of a mincer twice and then through a sieve into a bowl which has been set over ice. When well chilled, add the cream slowly and then the diced apricot, garlic and basil.

To stuff the loin, cut into two pieces and then down the centre, opening it out from the middle. Gently flatten it between cling film until the meat is about 1.5 cm/$\frac{5}{8}$ inch thick. Season and then pipe down the centre the ready prepared farce (stuffing). Bring the two pieces together and wrap in some blanched leek which has been thickly spread with veal farce. Finally, roll in the crepinette and chill until needed.

Strain the lamb stock and reduce until about a 600 ml/1 pint remains. Add the finely chopped tarragon, and if necessary, bind with a little fécule (cornflour) and cold water. Cook for a further 2–3 minutes before serving.

Sauté the stuffed loin of lamb in clarified butter, firstly on top of the stove and then in a hot oven (220°C, 425°F, Gas Mark 7) for about 10–15 minutes. Rest for 2–3 minutes before slicing. It is important that the stuffing is just cooked and at the same time the lamb remains pink.

A little compôte of tomato may be used for a base on which to sit the lamb for serving, using the freshly cooked mangetout as garnish. Serve with the Tarragon sauce, Charlotte of Aubergine and Glazed Schupfnudeln (see recipes below).

CHARLOTTE OF AUBERGINE

2 medium aubergines
1 medium-sized onion, peeled and diced
100 g/4 oz butter
$\frac{1}{4}$ garlic clove, peeled and chopped
25 g/1 oz fennel seeds
500 g/1 lb 4 oz button mushrooms, washed
pâté seasoning (a special seasoning using a
* selection of herbs and spices, ground*
* finely, to enhance the flavour of the dish)*
100 g/4 oz cubed aubergine, without skin

Butter well 4 small timbale moulds.

Cut 4 slices of aubergine 1 cm/$\frac{1}{2}$ inch thick and cut into rounds, using a round cutter. Pan-fry on both sides and leave to cool. (NB: it is important that the frying pan is only wiped out with clarified butter, otherwise the aubergines will become too soggy.) Prepare more aubergine pieces for the sides of the timbale moulds, but cutting them into finger lengths, instead of rounds. Once cool, use the aubergine pieces to line the base and sides of the buttered moulds.

Sauté the onion in butter until golden. Add the garlic and fennel seeds. In a separate frying pan, season the mushrooms with pâté seasoning and fry in as little fat as possible. Pass through the Rotocoup and season again if necessary.

Take the cubes of aubergine, and fry them quickly. Drain and add to the basic mixture.

Fill each charlotte (i.e. the aubergine-lined timbale moulds) with the mixture to the top. About 20 minutes before the charlottes are to be served, poach them in a water bath.

SCHUPFNUDELN

1 kg/2 lb potatoes
75 g/3 oz butter
2 eggs, beaten
190 g/6$\frac{1}{2}$ oz plain flour
salt and black pepper
grated nutmeg

Cook the potatoes and dry them out in the oven for 5 to 10 minutes until most of the moisture has evaporated. Pass through a potato press on to knobs of the butter. Cool and then add the lightly beaten egg and the sieved flour. Season with salt, pepper and nutmeg, and carefully mix together.

Taking 100 g/4 oz of the mixture at a time, roll into sausage shapes using cornflour and then cut into smaller pieces of about 10 g/$\frac{1}{4}$ oz in weight. Roll into small shapes.

Cook in simmering salt water with the addition of a little cornflour so that the schupfnudeln are held in suspension while cooking. As soon as they begin to float, cook them gently for 1 minute before removing with a slotted spoon into ice water.

Place on a tray with a dry cloth and leave for about two hours in the fridge.

To serve, sauté in fresh butter and finish in the oven until double in volume and golden brown.

Illustrated on page 118   SERVES 4

BEEF and VEAL

TERIYAKI BEEF KEBABS

750 g/1½ lb rump steak
5 tablespoons soy sauce
3 tablespoons medium sherry
3 tablespoons oil
2 garlic cloves, peeled and crushed
2.5 cm/1 inch piece fresh root ginger,
*   peeled and grated*
2 tablespoons soft brown sugar
1 large red pepper
2 medium-sized onions, peeled

Cut the beef into cubes of about 2.5 cm/1 inch and put into a bowl.

Combine the soy sauce, sherry, oil, garlic, ginger and sugar and mix well together. Pour over the beef and toss thoroughly. Cover and leave to marinate for at least 4 hours, and preferably overnight.

Halve the pepper, remove and discard the seeds and cut into 2.5 cm/1 inch squares.

Blanch the onions in boiling water for 5 minutes, drain and cool; then cut into wedges through the roots so the layers stay together.

Lift the beef from the marinade and thread on to four long skewers, alternating with the pepper and pieces of onion.

Cook under a moderately hot grill for about 5 minutes each side or until cooked as you like; or cook on a preheated barbecue for about the same time. Serve hot with salads.

SERVES 4

LEFT Loin of Jacob lamb stuffed with
apricots, basil and garlic (see pages 116–17)

STUFFED GREEN PEPPERS

450 g/1 lb raw minced beef
2 onions, peeled and finely chopped
50 g/2 oz frozen peas
50–100 g/2–4 oz frozen sweetcorn
salt and black pepper
4 green peppers
50 g/2 oz brown or white rice, boiled
300 ml/½ pint beef stock

Preheat the oven to moderately hot (190°C, 375°F, gas Mark 5).

Fry the mince in a saucepan with no extra fat for about 5 minutes, stirring from time to time, until the fat runs. Drain off any excess fat.

Add the onion, peas, sweetcorn and seasonings and continue cooking for about 10 minutes, again stirring from time to time.

Cut the tops off the green peppers and remove the seeds with a teaspoon; or cut in half lengthwise and scoop out the seeds.

Put the peppers in a bowl, cover with boiling water and leave for 5 minutes; then drain thoroughly.

Add the rice and half the stock to the mince mixture and blend well. Use to fill the peppers.

Stand the peppers in an ovenproof dish and surround with the rest of the stock. Cover and cook in the preheated oven for about 25 minutes.

SERVES 4

BEEF WITH MUSHROOMS AND CUMIN

750 g/1½ lb chuck or blade steak in one
*   piece*
salt and black pepper
1 tablespoon oil
2 large onions, peeled and thinly sliced
3–4 carrots, peeled and sliced
1–2 garlic cloves, peeled and crushed
300 ml/½ pint tomato juice
1 teaspoon cumin seeds
100 g/4 oz button mushrooms, trimmed
chopped parsley, to garnish

Preheat the oven to cool (150°C, 300°F, Gas Mark 2).

Trim the beef and cut into four even-sized portions. Season lightly with salt and pepper, if liked.

Heat the oil in a pan and fry the pieces of steak until well sealed on both sides; transfer to a casserole.

Fry the onions in the same fat for a few minutes and then add to the casserole with the carrots and garlic.

Bring the tomato juice to the boil, add the cumin seeds, season well and pour into the casserole.

Cover the casserole tightly and cook in the preheated oven for 2 hours. Add the mushrooms and cook for a further 30 minutes until the beef is very tender. Serve garnished with chopped parsley.

SERVES 4

BOILED BEEF AND CARROTS

1.5–1.75 kg/3–4 lb salted silverside or
    salted lean boned and rolled brisket
1 tablespoon brown sugar
2 bay leaves
8 whole cloves
water to cover
12 small onions, peeled
6 carrots, peeled and halved
2–3 sticks celery, cut into 10 cm/4 inch
    lengths
1 turnip, peeled and quartered

Dumplings
100 g/4 oz self-raising flour
pinch of salt
½ teaspoon mixed herbs
50 g/2 oz shredded suet
water to mix

Place the silverside or brisket in a saucepan and add the sugar, bay leaves, cloves and sufficient water to just cover.

Bring up to the boil and remove the scum that forms. Cover the pan and simmer gently for 2 hours.

Add the vegetables to the meat. Re-cover and continue cooking for about 45 minutes.

For the dumplings: sift the flour and salt into a bowl and mix in the herbs and suet. Add sufficient water to give an elastic dough. Divide into 12 small pieces and roll into balls.

About 15 minutes before the end of cooking time, place the dumplings on top of the meat and vegetables. Cover and continue cooking for about 15 minutes until the dumplings swell and rise to the top of the pan.

To serve: remove the dumplings with a slotted spoon to a dish; and remove the vegetables to another dish. Place the well drained meat on a serving dish.

The juices may be served as they are with the meat and vegetables or 600 ml/1 pint may be boiled hard to reduce by about a third before serving with the meat.

SERVES 4–6

BEEF STROGANOFF WITH TARRAGON

450 g/1 lb rump or fillet steak
1 tablespoon oil
1 large onion, peeled and thinly sliced
1–2 garlic cloves, peeled and crushed
175 g/6 oz button mushrooms, trimmed
    and thinly sliced
2–3 tablespoons white wine or cider or beef
    stock
salt and black pepper
½ teaspoon Worcestershire sauce
150 ml/¼ pint soured cream
1 tablespoon freshly chopped tarragon

To garnish
sprigs of fresh tarragon
cherry tomatoes

Trim the steak and cut into narrow strips.

Heat the oil in a large frying pan and fry the onion and garlic until soft but only very lightly coloured. Push to one side of the pan.

Add the strips of steak and cook quickly until just sealed.

Add the mushrooms and mix in with the steak and onions, cooking only for a minute or two.

Add the wine, or cider, or stock, plenty of seasonings and the Worcestershire sauce and heat for a few minutes.

Stir in the soured cream and reheat gently, stirring all the time, then mix in the tarragon.

Serve with freshly boiled pasta or rice, garnished with cherry tomatoes and fresh tarragon.

SERVES 4

CARBONADE OF BEEF

750 g/1½ lb best braising or chuck steak,
    cut into 2.5 cm/1 inch cubes
3 tablespoons oil
2–3 onions, peeled and sliced
2 garlic cloves, peeled and crushed
2–3 tablespoons plain flour
2 teaspoons brown sugar
300 ml/½ pint brown ale
300 ml/½ pint beef stock
salt and black pepper
2 tablespoons wine vinegar
1 bouquet garni
1 teaspoon French mustard
100 g/4 oz button mushrooms, trimmed
    and halved, if large

To garnish
4–6 slices French bread
little butter
parsley, to garnish

Preheat the oven to moderate (160°C, 325°F, Gas Mark 3).

Trim the beef if necessary. Heat 2 tablespoons of the oil in a pan and brown the cubes of meat all over; then transfer to a casserole.

Fry the onions and garlic in the same fat, adding a little more oil if necessary, until lightly browned. Transfer to the casserole.

Stir the flour into the pan juices and cook for 1–2 minutes then add the sugar followed by the ale and stock and bring up to the boil. Season well, add the vinegar, bouquet garni, French mustard and mushrooms and simmer for a minute or so.

Pour into the casserole and cover very tightly. Cook in the preheated very moderate oven for 2–2¼ hours until very tender.

Just before the casserole is ready, spread the slices of bread lightly with butter and put under a fairly low grill until just lightly browned and crisp.

Serve the casserole topped with the slices of bread and garnished with sprigs of fresh parsley.

SERVES 4–6

BEEF OLIVES WITH HAZELNUT STUFFING

4 thin slices topside of beef, beaten very thinly
salt and black pepper
1 tablespoon oil
1 onion, peeled and very finely chopped
50 g/2 oz hazelnuts, skinned and chopped
1–2 sticks celery, chopped
8 stuffed olives, chopped
50 g/2 oz fresh breadcrumbs
1 tablespoon freshly chopped parsley
1 egg, beaten
1 tablespoon plain flour
150 ml/¼ pint cider
150 ml/¼ pint beef stock

To garnish
parsley sprigs
4 tablespoons soured cream or natural yogurt

Preheat the oven to moderate (180°C, 350°F, Gas Mark 4).

Trim the slices of beef, if necessary, and season lightly.

Heat the oil in a pan and fry the onion gently until soft. Add the hazelnuts and celery and continue to fry until lightly browned. Turn into a bowl.

Add the olives, breadcrumbs, parsley and seasonings and bind together with the egg. Divide the stuffing among the slices of beef and roll up neatly, securing with wooden cocktail sticks or fine string.

Heat the rest of the oil in a pan and fry the olives until well browned all over. Transfer to a shallow casserole.

Stir the flour into the oil in the pan and cook for a minute or two then gradually add the cider and stock and bring up to the boil. Season well and pour over the olives.

Cover tightly and cook in a moderate oven for 1–1¼ hours until tender.

Remove the cocktail sticks or string from the olives and serve garnished with parsley and soured cream or yogurt.

SERVES 4

RED HOT BEEF PIE

750 g/1½ lb braising or stewing steak
2 tablespoons oil
2 onions, peeled and sliced
1 × 425 g/15 oz can peeled tomatoes
1½ teaspoons curry powder
2 teaspoons tomato purée
2 tablespoons wine vinegar
2 tablespoons apricot jam or redcurrant jelly
150 ml/¼ pint tomato juice
150 ml/¼ pint beef stock
salt and black pepper
1 bay leaf

Shortcrust pastry
225 g/8 oz plain white or granary flour
pinch of salt
50 g/2 oz butter or margarine
50 g/2 oz lard or white fat
cold water, to mix
beaten egg or top of the milk, to glaze

Preheat the oven to moderate (160°C, 325°F, Gas Mark 3).

Cut the beef into narrow strips. Heat the oil in a pan and fry the meat until well sealed. Add the onions and continue for 4–5 minutes.

Add the rest of the ingredients for the filling and bring up to the boil, stirring frequently.

Transfer to a casserole, cover tightly and cook in the preheated oven for about 2 hours or until tender, adding a little boiling water if getting too dry.

Adjust the seasonings, discard the bay leaf and turn the filling into a pie dish with a funnel in the centre and allow to cool.

For the pastry: sift the flour (not the granary flour) into a bowl with the salt and rub in the fats until the mixture resembles fine breadcrumbs. Add sufficient water to mix to a pliable dough.

Roll out the pastry about 5 cm/2 inch larger than the top of the pie dish and cut out a strip of almost 2.5 cm/1 inch wide; damp the rim of the dish and position the pastry strip on it.

Brush the pastry rim with water and position the lid, pressing the edges well together. Trim the edges, then flake and crimp. Roll out pastry trimmings and use to cut out leaves.

Brush the top of the pie with beaten egg or milk and make a hole in the centre over the funnel for the steam to escape. Decorate around the funnel and hole with pastry leaves and then glaze again with beaten egg or milk.

Cook in a fairly hot oven (200°C, 400°F, Gas Mark 6) for about 45 minutes until the pastry is a good golden brown and the contents piping hot.

SERVES 4–6

CHILLI CASSOULET

450 g/1 lb lean minced beef
2 onions, peeled and sliced
1 garlic clove, peeled and crushed
2 tablespoons oil
1 × 425 g/15 oz can red kidney beans,
  drained
1 × 225 g/8 oz can baked beans
1 teaspoon chilli powder
salt and black pepper
250 ml/scant ½ pint beef stock
1 tablespoon cornflour
chopped parsley or mixed herbs, to garnish

Preheat the oven to moderate (160°C, 325°F, Gas Mark 3).

Fry the lean minced beef in the heated oil to seal and then transfer to an ovenproof casserole.

Fry the onions and garlic in the same fat until lightly coloured; transfer to the casserole.

Add the beans to the casserole.

Put the chilli powder, seasonings and stock into the pan and bring up to the boil. Pour over the meat in the casserole and cover tightly.

Cook in the preheated oven for 1 hour.

Blend the cornflour with 2 tablespoons of water and stir into the casserole. Return to the oven for about 20–30 minutes.

Serve very hot generously sprinkled with parsley or mixed herbs.

SERVES 4

Chilli cassoulet

STEAK AND KIDNEY PUDDING

Suet crust pastry
225 g/8 oz self raising flour
½ teaspoon salt
75–100 g/3–4 oz shredded suet
approx. 150 ml/¼ pint water to mix

Filling
450 g/1 lb best chuck or braising steak
175 g/6 oz ox kidney or 2–3 lambs' kidneys
2 tablespoons well seasoned plain flour
100 g/4 oz mushrooms, sliced or quartered
salt and black pepper
4 tablespoons stock, water or wine
parsley, to garnish

For the pastry: sift the flour and salt into a bowl and mix in the suet. Add sufficient water to mix to a fairly soft dough. Knead lightly. Roll out three-quarters of the pastry on a floured surface and use to line a greased 900 ml/1½ pint pudding basin.

Cut the steak into 2 cm/¾ inch pieces, discarding any fat or gristle, and cut the skinned and cored kidney into pieces half the size. Toss the meats in the flour.

Spoon the meats into the lined basin alternating with the mushrooms and seasonings until almost full. Add the stock, water or wine.

Roll out the remaining pastry to form a lid, damp the edges and position, pressing the edges firmly together.

Cover first with a layer of greased greaseproof paper with a pleat across the centre and then either a pudding cloth or a pleated foil lid, tying very securely under the rim of the basin.

Stand the basin in a saucepan with boiling water coming half way up the side of the basin, or in the top of a steamer. Cover and simmer gently for about 4 hours, adding more boiling water to the saucepan as necessary.

To serve: remove the cloth or foil and greaseproof paper and tie a cloth around the side of the basin and garnish with parsley.

SERVES 4

STEAKS WITH WHISKY

4 steaks – fillet, sirloin or rump – approx.
*   100–175 g/4–6 oz each*
salt and black pepper
1 garlic clove, peeled and crushed
25 g/1 oz butter
1 teaspoon oil
4 tablespoons whisky
1 teaspoon Worcestershire sauce
4 tablespoons single cream
freshly chopped tarragon, to garnish

Trim the steaks, if necessary, season lightly and rub all over with garlic.

Heat the butter and oil in a large frying pan and add the rest of the garlic. When hot add the steaks and fry quickly to seal on both sides. Continue to cook for 1–3 minutes each side until cooked to your liking.

Add the whisky and Worcestershire sauce and bring to the boil. Season well and then stir in the cream. Reheat gently.

Serve at once, sprinkled with tarragon.

SERVES 4

POT ROAST STUFFED VEAL

1.25–1.5 kg/2½–3 lb veal shoulder, boned

Stuffing
1 tablespoon oil
1 onion, peeled and chopped
2 rashers bacon, derinded and chopped
1 garlic clove, peeled and crushed
50 g/2 oz chopped peanuts
1 tablespoon freshly chopped parsley
1 teaspoon dried oregano or marjoram
1 dessert apple, cored and coarsely grated
75 g/3 oz fresh breadcrumbs
salt and black pepper
1 egg, beaten
300 ml/½ pint cider or stock
2 teaspoons cornflour
2 teaspoons tomato purée
good dash of Worcestershire sauce

To garnish
parsley or watercress
fried button mushrooms

Preheat the oven to moderate (180°C, 350°F, Gas Mark 4).

Unroll the veal, if necessary, and trim. For the stuffing: heat the oil and fry the bacon, onion and garlic until soft. Add the peanuts and continue for a few minutes. Turn into a bowl.

Add the herbs, apple, breadcrumbs and plenty of seasonings and bind together with beaten egg.

Spread the stuffing over the inside of the joint and roll up carefully. Secure with skewers and string and if possible remove the skewers.

Stand the veal joint in a roasting tin or large casserole and season lightly. If liked, brush with a little oil or melted fat. Pour the cider or stock over and around the veal and cover with foil.

Cook in the preheated oven for an hour. Remove the foil and baste with the juices. Cook for 30 minutes, baste again and continue cooking for a further 30 minutes until tender.

Strain off the juices and make up to 300 ml/½ pint with stock or water. Thicken with cornflour blended with a little cold water, stir in the tomato purée and Worcestershire sauce and simmer for 1–2 minutes. Adjust the seasonings and strain into a sauce boat.

Remove the joint to a serving dish and garnish with parsley or watercress and fried mushrooms. Serve in slices with the sauce.

SERVES 4–6

VEAL AND TARRAGON PIE

1 large onion, peeled and sliced
2 tablespoons oil
750 g/1½ lb pie veal, cubed
25 g/1 oz plain flour
150 ml/¼ pint dry white wine or cider
300 ml/½ pint veal or chicken stock
salt and black pepper
grated rind of 1 small lemon
1 tablespoon lemon juice
100 g/4 oz mushrooms, trimmed and sliced
1 tablespoon freshly chopped tarragon or
*   1½ teaspoons dried tarragon*

Pastry
175 g/6 oz granary flour
pinch of salt
40 g/1½ oz butter or margarine
40 g/1½ oz lard or white fat
cold water, to mix
beaten egg or top of the milk, to glaze

Preheat the oven to moderate (160°C, 325°F, Gas Mark 3).

Fry the onion gently in the heated cooking oil until soft. Add the veal and continue cooking until well sealed all over.

Stir in the flour and cook for a minute or so and then gradually add the wine or cider and stock and bring up to the boil.

Add the lemon rind, juice, mushrooms, and tarragon and simmer for 1–2 minutes. Season well and transfer to a casserole.

Cover tightly and cook in the preheated oven for about an hour or until tender. Pour into a pie dish and leave until cold.

For the pastry: put the flour and salt into a bowl and rub in the fats until the mixture resembles fine breadcrumbs. Add sufficient cold water to mix to a pliable dough.

Roll out thinly, cut a strip about 2 cm/¾ inch wide and place on the dampened rim of the dish. Roll the rest to fit the top of the pie, damp the pastry rim and position the lid, pressing the edges well together.

Trim the edges and then flake with a knife, and crimp. Brush with beaten egg or milk and make a hole in the centre.

Roll out the pastry trimmings and cut out leaves and use to decorate around the central hole. Glaze again and cook in a fairly hot oven (200°C, 400°F, Gas Mark 6) for about 40–45 minutes or until the pastry is well browned and the filling piping hot.
SERVES 4–6

OSSO BUCO

8 pieces shin of veal (approx 1.25–1.5
*   kg/2½–3 lb)*
2 tablespoons oil
1–2 onions, peeled and sliced
2 garlic cloves, peeled and crushed
4 sticks celery, sliced
2–3 carrots, peeled and cut into sticks
150 ml/¼ pint dry white wine
300 ml/½ pint chicken or veal stock
salt and black pepper
1 × 425 g/15 oz can peeled tomatoes
1 bay leaf
½ teaspoon dried oregano (optional)
1 tablespoon cornflour (optional)

Preheat the oven to moderate (160°C, 325°F, Gas Mark 3).

Trim the meat free of any chips of bone. Heat the oil in a large pan and fry the pieces of meat all over to lightly brown and seal. Transfer to a large casserole.

Fry the onions and garlic gently for 4–5 minutes until soft, but not coloured. Add the celery and carrots and continue for a few minutes.

Add the wine, stock, seasonings, tomatoes, bay leaf and oregano, if used, and bring up to the boil. Pour over the veal and cover tightly.

Cook in a very moderate oven for about 2½ hours or until the meat is very tender.

Discard the bay leaf, taste and adjust the seasonings and, if liked, thicken the juices with cornflour blended in a little cold water. Bring back to the boil before serving.
SERVES 4

VEAL ESCALOPES WITH CUCUMBER DRESSING

4 veal escalopes (100–150 g/4–5 oz each)
little seasoned plain flour
1 egg, beaten
approx 100 g/4 oz fresh white
*   breadcrumbs*
oil for shallow frying

Cucumber dressing
150 ml/¼ pint thick set natural yogurt
about ⅓ cucumber, coarsely grated
1 tablespoon freshly chopped mint or 1
*   teaspoon dried mint*
good pinch of grated lemon rind
1 tablespoon chopped chives or spring
*   onions*

To garnish
lemon wedges
watercress
spring onions

Trim the veal, if necessary, and dip first into the flour, shaking off all the excess.

Next dip in beaten egg and coat thoroughly in breadcrumbs, pressing them well on. At this stage the escalopes may be chilled for 2–3 hours.

For the dressing: combine all the ingredients, adding a little salt and pepper, if liked, and turn into a bowl. Cover and leave to stand for 2 hours or so if possible before serving.

When ready to cook; heat the oil or fat in a frying pan and when fairly hot fry the escalopes for 4–5 minutes on each side until golden brown and cooked through.

Drain very thoroughly on crumpled kitchen paper and serve quickly with a garnish of lemon, watercress and spring onions and with the dressing in a bowl.
SERVES 4

LAMB

LANCASHIRE HOTPOT

8–12 middle neck of lamb chops or best end
of neck chops
225 g/8 oz onions, peeled and thinly sliced
4 carrots, peeled and sliced
2 lambs' kidneys, skinned, halved, cored
and diced (optional)
salt and black pepper
½ teaspoon mixed herbs
750 g/1½ lb potatoes, peeled and sliced
300 ml/½ pint good stock
25 g/1 oz butter or margarine, melted
chopped parsley, to garnish

Preheat the oven to moderate (160°C, 325°F, Gas Mark 3).

Remove any excess fat from the chops and layer them in a large casserole with the onions, carrots, kidneys, seasonings and herbs.

Cover the contents of the casserole with a thick layer of overlapping slices of potato.

Bring the stock up to the boil and pour over the potatoes and then brush them liberally with melted butter or margarine.

Cover the casserole with a lid or foil and cook in the preheated oven for 2 hours.

Remove the lid from the casserole, increase the oven temperature to hot (220°C, 425°F, Gas Mark 7), and continue for about 20 minutes or so until the potatoes are well browned. Sprinkle with chopped parsley and serve.

SERVES 4

LAMB IN ORANGE AND MINT

4 boneless lamb leg steaks or double loin
chops
grated rind and juice of 2 oranges
salt and black pepper
3 tablespoons freshly chopped mint
little oil
1½ teaspoons plain flour
4–6 tablespoons stock

To garnish
fresh sprigs of mint
orange wedges

Place the lamb in a shallow dish and sprinkle first with the orange rind, then juice, a little salt and pepper and then the chopped mint.

Turn the lamb in the marinade and leave in a cool place for at least 30 minutes.

When ready to cook, drain the meat well, reserving the marinade and brush lightly with oil. Stand on a grill rack in the grill pan.

Cook under a preheated moderate grill for about 7 minutes each side until well browned and just cooked through. Remove and keep warm.

Transfer the pan juices and a little of the fat to a saucepan and stir in the flour. Cook for a minute or so and then gradually add the marinade and stock and bring up to the boil. Season to taste and serve poured over the chops, garnished with mint and orange wedges.

SERVES 4

LAMB CASSEROLE WITH CUMIN

750 g/1½ lb lean lamb (leg or shoulder)
2 onions, peeled and sliced
4 carrots, peeled and cut into thin strips
2 sticks celery, cut into strips
300 ml/½ pint tomato juice
2 teaspoons ground cumin
1 garlic clove, peeled and crushed
salt and black pepper
100 g/4 oz mushrooms, trimmed and sliced
50 g/2 oz frozen peas

Preheat the oven to moderate (160°C, 325°F, Gas Mark 3).

Trim the lamb of any excess fat and cut into 2.5 cm/1 inch cubes.

Put the lamb, onions, carrots and celery into a casserole and mix well.

Put the tomato juice into a saucepan with the cumin, garlic and seasonings and bring slowly up to the boil.

Pour over the lamb, mix well and cover tightly. Cook in the preheated oven for 1 hour.

Add the mushrooms and peas to the casserole, mix well, re-cover and cook for a further hour.

Serve with boiled rice, pasta or boiled potatoes.

Illustrated on page 130 SERVES 4

RACK OF LAMB WITH REDCURRANT AND PORT SAUCE

1 rack of lamb, (8 cutlets in a joint)
1 garlic clove, peeled and sliced thinly
8–10 small sprigs fresh rosemary

Sauce
1 lemon
225 g/8 oz redcurrant jelly
3–4 tablespoons port
1 teaspoon arrowroot
2 teaspoons cold water
fresh rosemary, to garnish

Preheat the oven to moderate (180°C, 350°F, Gas Mark 4).

Using a sharp knife, make 8–10 slits into the outside surface of the lamb fat and insert a sliver of garlic and sprig of rosemary into each.

Stand the joint on a rack in a roasting tin and cook in the centre of the preheated oven for about an hour.

Meanwhile for the sauce: pare the rind thinly from the lemon with a potato peeler and cut into thin strips.

Squeeze the juice from the lemon and put into a small pan with 100 ml/4 fl oz water and the lemon rind strips and bring to the boil; simmer for 5 minutes until tender.

Add the redcurrant jelly and heat gently until dissolved and then stir in the port.

Blend the arrowroot with the water, stir into the sauce and heat until thickened.

Serve the lamb with the sauce, garnished with fresh rosemary.

SERVES 4

LEFT Lamb casserole with cumin (see page 129); BELOW Rack of lamb with redcurrant and port sauce

STUFFED BREAST OF LAMB

2 breasts of lamb, boned
salt and black pepper

Stuffing
1 tablespoon oil
1 onion, peeled and finely chopped
2 sticks celery, chopped
75 g/3 oz soft brown breadcrumbs
50 g/2 oz walnut halves, chopped
1 dessert apple, cored and coarsely grated
1 teaspoon curry powder
grated rind of ½ lemon
1 egg, beaten

Sauce
25 g/1 oz plain flour
300 ml/½ pint cider
150 ml/¼ pint stock
celery leaves and/or parsley, to garnish

Preheat the oven to hot (220°C, 425°F, Gas Mark 7).

Trim off excess fat from the lamb and cut out any gristle or membrane. Cut each breast in half and season lightly.

For the stuffing: heat the oil in a pan and fry the onion and celery very gently until soft. Turn into a bowl and mix in the breadcrumbs, walnuts, apple, curry powder and lemon rind. Season well and bind together with the egg.

Divide the stuffing among the pieces of lamb, spreading it out evenly to cover the inside, then roll up each carefully and secure with wooden cocktail sticks or tie with fine string.

Place in a greased roasting tin and roast without adding any further fat, in the preheated oven for 50–60 minutes until well browned and cooked through. Baste several times during cooking with the fat which emerges from the joints.

Remove from the tin to a serving dish and keep warm. Spoon off all but 2 tablespoons fat from the pan, stir in the flour and cook for a minute or so, stirring frequently. Gradually add the cider and stock and simmer for 3–4 minutes. Adjust the seasonings and strain into a sauce boat.

Serve the rolls garnished with celery leaves and/or parsley after removing the cocktail sticks or string.

SERVES 4

LAMB AND CAPER PASTIES

225 g/8 oz plain flour
pinch of salt
50 g/2 oz butter or margarine
50 g/2 oz lard or white fat
water, to mix

Filling
225 g/8 oz lean raw lamb, minced
1 small onion, peeled and finely chopped
salt and black pepper
2 tablespoons capers, chopped
1 carrot, peeled and coarsely grated
1 tablespoon freshly chopped parsley
beaten egg, to glaze

Preheat the oven to moderately hot (200°C, 400°F, Gas Mark 6).

Sift the flour with a pinch of salt into a bowl and rub in the fats until the mixture resembles fine breadcrumbs. Add sufficient water to mix to a pliable dough.

Combine the lamb, onion, seasonings, capers, carrot and parsley. Divide into four.

Roll out the pastry and cut out four circles of approx. 18 cm/7 inch in diameter. Place a portion of meat in the centre of each circle.

Damp the pastry edges with water and bring together at the top to form a pasty. Press the edges well together and crimp.

Stand on a lightly greased baking sheet and glaze the pasties thoroughly with beaten egg.

Cook in the preheated oven for 35–40 minutes until well browned. Serve hot, warm or cold.

SERVES 4

AUBERGINE MOUSSAKA

2 aubergines
salt and black pepper
450 g/1 lb lean lamb, minced (use leg, shoulder or fillet)
2 large onions, peeled and thinly sliced
1–2 garlic cloves, peeled and crushed
225 g/8 oz peeled tomatoes
2 tablespoons tomato purée
1 teaspoon Worcestershire sauce
1 teaspoon dried oregano

Topping
2 eggs
150 ml/¼ pint single cream
chopped parsley, to garnish (optional)

Wipe and trim the aubergines and cut into slices about 2 cm/¾ inch thick. Place on a board or tray and sprinkle liberally with salt. Leave for 30 minutes then rinse off under cold running water and drain very thoroughly.

Arrange the slices of aubergine over the base and up the sides of a casserole.

Put the minced lamb into a heavy-based saucepan with the onions and cook gently until the fat runs, stirring from time to time. Cook for about 5 minutes then stir in the tomatoes, purée, Worcestershire sauce and oregano.

Bring up to the boil, season well and pour into the casserole.

Cook in a preheated moderate oven (180°C, 350°F, Gas Mark 4) for about 45 minutes until cooked through.

Beat the eggs and cream together, season and pour over the meat and aubergines. Return to the oven, still uncovered, and cook for a further 15–20 minutes until the custard has set and is lightly browned. If liked, the dish may be sprinkled with chopped parsley before serving.

SERVES 4

STUFFED GUARD OF HONOUR

2 best ends of neck

Stuffing
1 tablespoon oil
1 onion, peeled and very finely chopped
1 garlic clove, peeled and crushed
50 g/2 oz no-need-to-soak apricots, finely chopped
40 g/1½ oz toasted hazelnuts, finely chopped
2 tablespoons freshly chopped dill or 1 tablespoon dried dillweed
75 g/3 oz long-grain rice, freshly boiled
salt and black pepper
1 egg, beaten
fresh dill to garnish

If making the guard of honour yourself, buy two best ends of neck of lamb and trim the bones clean of meat and fat for about 6 cm/2½ inches. Place the two pieces of lamb together and fold so the bones are criss-crossed at the top. The skin should be outside and they should be sewn together at the base. Once stuffed the joint can also be tied into place during cooking if it tends to stand unevenly.

Preheat the oven to moderately hot (200°C, 400°F, Gas Mark 6).

For the stuffing: heat the oil in a pan and fry the onion and garlic until soft. Turn into a bowl and mix in the apricots, hazelnuts, dill, rice and seasonings and bind together with the egg.

Stand the guard of honour in a roasting tin and undo. Place the stuffing in the centre and reassemble. Tie with string, if necessary. Protect the tips of the bones with foil.

Cook in the preheated oven for 50–60 minutes until cooked through and well browned on the outside.

Serve on a platter, garnished with fresh dill and with a cutlet frill on top of each chop bone. Use the pan juices to make a gravy. Redcurrant jelly may also be served.

SERVES 5–6

MINCED LAMB KEBABS
(*MICROWAVE RECIPE*)

450 g/1 lb lean lamb, minced
1 onion, peeled and very finely chopped
1 tablespoon freshly chopped parsley
salt
1 teaspoon ground cumin
2 teaspoons paprika
pinch of cayenne
pinch of ground cinnamon
2 teaspoons soy sauce

NOTE: instructions for 500 watt ovens are given in brackets.

Mix together the lamb, onion, parsley, a pinch of salt, and spices and divide into 8 portions.

Shape each piece into a sausage about 10 cm/4 inches long around 8 wooden skewers. Chill for 30 minutes.

Place on a microwave roasting rack and brush all over with soy sauce. Cover with a slit roasting bag.

Cook on 75% for 7–9 minutes (High 7–9 minutes) or until the lamb is cooked.

Serve on a bed of freshly boiled rice with a salad.

SERVES 4

CURRIED LAMB

1.25 kg/2½ lb middle neck of lamb
1 tablespoon ground coriander
1 teaspoon turmeric
½ teaspoon ground cumin
¼ teaspoon chilli powder
¼ teaspoon ground cinnamon
pinch of ground cloves
1½ teaspoons garam masala
2 tablespoons oil
2 large onions, peeled and sliced
1–2 garlic cloves, peeled and crushed
450 ml/¾ pint stock
salt
150 ml/¼ pint plain, unsweetened yogurt

Accompaniments
sliced tomatoes and sliced onions
sliced banana dipped in lemon juice
poppadums
mango chutney or lime pickle

Trim the lamb and cut into small chops and pieces.

Combine the spices, and garam masala.

Heat the oil in a pan and fry the onions and garlic until lightly browned, then stir in the curry spices and cook gently for 2–3 minutes.

Add the lamb and cook gently for about 15 minutes, stirring frequently.

Add the stock and bring up to the boil. Add salt to taste and either cover the pan and simmer very gently for 1½–2 hours until tender, adding extra stock, if necessary; or transfer to a large casserole, cover tightly and cook in a moderate oven (160°C, 325°F, Gas Mark 3) for 2 hours.

Either stir the yogurt through the curry or serve each portion with yogurt spooned on to it, and serve with freshly boiled rice and accompaniments.

SERVES 4

STUFFED SHOULDER OF LAMB

100 g/4 oz no-need-to-soak stoned prunes,
   chopped
1 onion, peeled and finely chopped
1 tablespoon oil
25 g/1 oz butter or margarine
finely grated rind of 1 orange
2 tablespoons freshly chopped parsley
salt and black pepper
½ teaspoon ground coriander
75 g/3 oz fresh breadcrumbs
1 egg, beaten
1.6 kg/3½ lb shoulder of lamb, boned and
   rolled
little oil
40 g/1½ oz plain flour
300 ml/½ pint apple juice
150 ml/¼ pint stock
watercress or fresh herbs, to garnish

Preheat the oven to hot (220°C, 425°F, Gas
Mark 7).

For the stuffing: put the prunes into a
bowl. Fry the onion gently in the heated oil
until soft and add to the prunes with the
orange rind, parsley, seasonings and coriander. Mix in the breadcrumbs and bind
together with beaten egg.

Unroll the lamb and spread the stuffing
evenly over the inside. Carefully reroll to
enclose the stuffing and secure with skewers and string. If possible then remove the
skewers.

Place the joint in a roasting tin and brush
lightly with oil. Season lightly and cook in
the preheated oven for about 2 hours (after
calculating the times from the chart on page
00). Baste at least once during cooking.

Remove the joint to a serving dish and
keep warm. Spoon off all but 2 tablespoons
fat from the roasting tin and stir in the flour.
Cook for a minute or so and then gradually
add the apple juice and stock and bring up
to the boil. Simmer for 2–3 minutes, adjust
the seasonings and strain into a sauce boat.

Serve the lamb, garnished with watercress or fresh herbs, with the gravy.

SERVES 4–6

POT ROAST LEG OF LAMB

225 g/8 oz haricot beans, soaked overnight
1 × 1.5–1.6 kg/3–3½ lb leg of lamb
4 garlic cloves, peeled and cut into slivers
2 teaspoons fresh rosemary
salt and black pepper
3 tablespoons oil
12–16 button onions, peeled
2 carrots, peeled and sliced
3–4 sticks celery, sliced
1 × 425 g/15 oz can peeled tomatoes
150 ml/¼ pint red wine
300 ml/½ pint stock
2 teaspoons Worcestershire sauce
2 bay leaves

Drain the beans and put into a saucepan of
clean water, bring to the boil, skim and
simmer for an hour.

Make deep incisions all over the lamb
and insert slivers of garlic into them. Rub
the rosemary into the lamb and season well.

Heat the oil in a pan and fry the joint all
over to brown and completely seal. Remove
from the pan.

Fry the onions in the same fat until
lightly browned.

Drain the beans and place in a large
casserole. Stand the lamb on the beans and
arrange the onions, carrots and celery
around it.

Heat the tomatoes with the wine, stock,
Worcestershire sauce, bay leaves and
plenty of seasoning and, when boiling, pour
over the beans.

Cover the casserole very tightly, adding a
sheet of foil under the lid if necessary and
cook in a preheated moderate oven (180°C,
350°F, Gas Mark 4) for 1¾–2 hours. Turn the
lamb over in the casserole at least twice
during the cooking.

Remove the lamb to a serving dish and
leave to set for 10 minutes or so.

Spoon off any fat from the surface of the
beans and serve some of these around the
joint and the rest separately, still in the
sauce to hand with the meat.

SERVES 4–6

LAMB STIR-FRY

450 g/1 lb boneless leg of lamb or fillet of
   lamb
3 tablespoons oil
1 garlic clove, peeled and crushed
6–8 spring onions, trimmed and sliced
3 carrots, peeled and sliced
2–3 sticks green celery, thinly sliced
3 courgettes, trimmed and sliced
50–100 g/2–4 oz white cabbage, finely
   shredded
salt and black pepper
2 teaspoons Worcestershire sauce
1 tablespoon soy sauce
4 tablespoons apple juice

Cut the lamb into thin strips, free of any fat
or gristle.

Heat the oil in a pan and fry the lamb for
5–6 minutes until well sealed and cooked
through. Remove from the pan and keep
warm.

Add the garlic, onions, carrots and celery
to the pan and fry in the same fat for about 5
minutes.

Add the courgettes and cabbage and
continue for a minute or so, stirring all the
time.

Add plenty of seasonings, the Worcestershire sauce, soy sauce and apple juice and
return the lamb to the pan.

Cook for 2–3 minutes, stirring frequently
and serve at once with freshly boiled
noodles or rice.

SERVES 4

NOTE: the carrots can be cut with an aspic
cutter to give interesting shapes.

RIGHT Lamb stir-fry

NOISETTES OF LAMB

4–8 noisettes of lamb
salt and black pepper
25 g/1 oz butter or margarine
1 tablespoon oil

Sauce
1 tablespoon oil
1 onion, peeled and thinly sliced
1 garlic clove, peeled and crushed
1 small red pepper, deseeded and thinly
*   sliced*
100 g/4 oz button mushrooms, trimmed
*   and sliced*
4 tablespoons red wine
1 teaspoon French mustard
good dash of Worcestershire sauce
2 teaspoons freshly chopped mint
4–8 slices toast, cut into rounds
fresh mint sprigs, to garnish

Trim the lamb and season lightly with salt and pepper, if liked.

For the sauce: heat the oil in a pan and fry the onion and garlic gently until soft but not coloured. Add the pepper and continue for 2–3 minutes until soft; then add the mushrooms and continue for a minute or so longer.

Add the wine, mustard and Worcestershire sauce and simmer for 2–3 minutes, then season well and stir in the mint.

Melt the butter and oil in a large frying pan and fry the noisettes for 5–8 minutes each side in a covered pan until cooked through. Alternatively, they may be cooked under a moderate grill for about 5 minutes each side.

Stand the rounds of toast on a serving dish and top each with a cooked noisette.

Reheat the sauce and spoon over and around the noisettes. Garnish with sprigs of mint.

NOTE: this recipe may also be used for all types of lamb chops or cutlets.

MUSTARD GLAZED LAMB CHOPS

4 double loin or chump chops
little oil
salt and black pepper
4 teaspoons wholegrain mustard
2 teaspoons soft brown sugar
watercress and cherry tomatoes, to garnish

Brush the lamb chops lightly with oil and, if liked, season lightly.

Cook under a preheated moderate grill for about 5–7 minutes depending on the thickness of the chops.

Turn the chops over and cook the second side for 2–3 minutes.

Mix the mustard and brown sugar together and spread evenly over the chops. Cook for a further 2–4 minutes until browned and just cooked through.

Serve at once, garnished with watercress and cherry tomatoes.

SERVES 4

LAMB AND AUBERGINE KEBABS

450 g/1 lb lean lamb
150 ml/¼ pint plain unsweetened yogurt
4 teaspoons hot curry paste
1 garlic clove, peeled and crushed
1 aubergine
3 tablespoons oil
225 g/8 oz long grain rice
salt and black pepper
1 teaspoon turmeric
50 g/2 oz blanched almonds, cut into slivers
*   and toasted*
50 g/2 oz sultanas

Trim the lamb and cut into cubes. Place in a bowl and add the yogurt, 2 teaspoons curry paste and the garlic. Mix well and cover.

Trim the stalk from the aubergine and cut into 2.5 cm/1 inch slices and then cut each into quarters. Cook in boiling water for 2 minutes and drain.

Mix the oil and remaining curry paste together in a bowl, add the warm aubergine and mix well. Cover.

Leave both lamb and aubergine to marinate for at least 4 hours and preferably overnight.

Cook the rice in plenty of boiling salted water with the turmeric added for about 12–14 minutes until tender. Drain thoroughly and mix in the almonds and sultanas. Turn into a bowl and keep warm.

Thread the pieces of lamb and aubergine alternately on to four long skewers and cook under a moderate grill for about 5 minutes each side until well browned and cooked through.

Alternatively, cook on a barbecue for about the same time.

Serve the kebabs on the yellow rice together with a salad.

SERVES 4

LAMB PICNIC PIE

350 g/12 oz shortcrust pastry (350 g/12 oz plain flour etc)
225 g/8 oz lean lamb, finely chopped
100 g/4 oz lean back bacon, derinded and chopped
1 onion, peeled and grated or finely chopped
salt and black pepper
1 × 200 g/7 oz can apricot halves, drained
150 ml/¼ pint stock
1 egg, beaten
2 teaspoons powdered gelatine
parsley, to garnish

Preheat the oven to moderately hot (200°C, 400°F, Gas Mark 6).

Make up the pastry as usual. Roll out two-thirds and use to line a greased and base-lined deep 20 cm/8 inch sandwich tin.

Combine the lamb, bacon, and onion and season very well. Place half of the meat in the pastry case.

Arrange the apricot halves over the meat and cover with the rest of the meat mixture. Spoon 4 tablespoons of the stock over the meat.

Roll out the remaining pastry to a circle to fit the tin. Position the lid, damping the edges with water. Press well together, trim and crimp.

Roll out the pastry trimmings and cut out leaves to decorate the top of the pie. Glaze thoroughly with beaten egg and make a hole in the centre of the pie.

Cook in the preheated oven for 45–50 minutes until golden brown and cooked.

Dissolve the gelatine in the remaining stock and season well. As the pie cools pour into the pie through a small funnel inserted in the central hole. Leave to cool, then chill.

Serve cold in slices with salads.

SERVES 6–8

ROAST CROWN OF LAMB

2 best ends of neck or 1 prepared crown

Stuffing
1–2 tablespoons oil
1 large onion, peeled and chopped
1 garlic clove, peeled and crushed
175 g/6 oz mushrooms, trimmed and chopped
1 teaspoon dried thyme
40 g/1½ oz pine nuts, toasted
50 g/2 oz fresh breadcrumbs
50 g/2 oz long-grain rice, freshly boiled
salt and black pepper
1–2 tablespoons freshly chopped parsley
1 egg, beaten
fresh herbs, to garnish

To make a crown of lamb take two best end of necks of lamb each with at least 6 cutlets. Remove the chine bones and scrape away the meat and fat from the tips of the bones to about 4 cm/1½ inch.

Place the joints back to back and sew together with the bones curving outwards to give a crown shape, using a trussing needle and fine string.

Preheat the oven to moderate (180°C, 350°F, Gas Mark 4).

For the stuffing: heat the oil in a pan and fry the onion and garlic gently until soft. Add the mushrooms and continue cooking for 2–3 minutes; turn into a bowl.

Add the thyme, pine nuts, breadcrumbs, rice, seasonings and parsley and bind together with the egg.

Stand the crown roast in a roasting tin and fill the centre with the stuffing, giving it a slightly domed top. Lay a piece of foil over the stuffing and protect each of the bones with foil.

Cook in the preheated oven, allowing about 1½ hours or until cooked through and well browned. Baste once or twice during cooking. Remove the foil from the stuffing for about the last 30 minutes of cooking time for it to crisp up.

To serve: stand the crown roast on a serving dish and top each bone tip with a cutlet frill. Garnish with fresh herbs.

Use the pan juices to make a gravy and serve with roast or new potatoes, peas and another green vegetable. Redcurrant jelly may also be served as an accompaniment.

SERVES 6

BARBECUE-STYLE LAMB RIBLETS

2 breasts of lamb, trimmed
2 tablespoons clear honey
2 tablespoons wine vinegar
2 tablespoons soy sauce
salt and black pepper

To garnish
shredded white cabbage or white lettuce
strips of red or orange pepper
raw button mushrooms, sliced

Cut the breasts of lamb into riblets through the gaps between the bones and then remove as much excess fat and membrane as possible.

Place in a dish or tin. Combine the honey, vinegar, soy sauce and a little seasoning and pour over the meat. Toss in the marinade and leave to stand for at least 3 hours and preferably overnight in the refrigerator.

When ready to cook, preheat the oven to moderately hot (190°C, 375°F, Gas Mark 5).

Remove the lamb from the refrigerator and place the riblets on a rack in a roasting tin and pour the rest of the marinade over them.

Cook in the preheated oven for about 50 minutes, basting once during cooking, until well browned and crispy.

Serve garnished with a mixture of shredded cabbage, pepper and mushrooms and with baked jacket potatoes.

SERVES 4

PORK and BACON

PORK AND ORANGE PÂTÉ

225 g/8 oz belly pork, derinded
225 g/8 oz lean pork, derinded
100 g/4 oz smoked bacon, derinded
50 g/2 oz fresh white breadcrumbs
1 onion, peeled and chopped
1 garlic clove, crushed
1 egg, beaten
grated rind and juice of 1 orange
1 tablespoon dry sherry
salt and black pepper

To garnish
orange slices
fresh bay leaves

Preheat the oven to moderate (180°C, 350°F, Gas Mark 4).

Finely chop or process or mince the two types of pork and the bacon.

Add the breadcrumbs, onion, garlic, egg, orange rind and juice, sherry and plenty of salt and freshly ground black pepper and mix thoroughly.

Turn the mixture into a greased 900 ml/1½ pint ovenproof dish or tin and level the top. Cover with greased foil.

Stand in a roasting tin with water coming halfway up the side of the dish and cook in the preheated oven for 1½ hours.

Cool and then cover with a weighted plate and chill overnight.

Serve the pâté garnished with orange slices and fresh bay leaves; cut into wedges and serve with crusty French bread rolls or crispbread.

SERVES 8

PORK TENDERLOIN WITH LEMON AND CHIVE SAUCE

450 g/1 lb pork tenderloin
4 tablespoons white wine
3 tablespoons oil
2 tablespoons lemon juice
2 bay leaves
salt and black pepper

Sauce
grated rind and juice of 1 lemon
1 tablespoon chopped chives
2 teaspoons cornflour
100 ml/4 fl oz single cream

Cut the pork tenderloin into 1 cm/½ inch slices.

Mix together the wine, 2 tablespoons oil, the lemon juice, bay leaves and seasonings for the marinade and add the pork. Coat thoroughly, cover and leave in a cool place for 1–2 hours.

When ready to cook, remove the pork from the marinade and dry. Heat the remaining oil in a large frying pan and cook the pieces of pork for about 3 minutes each side. Remove from the pan and keep warm.

In the same pan add the lemon rind and juice, chives and cornflour blended with the cream and heat gently, stirring continuously, until it thickens and comes just to the boil. Adjust the seasonings and pour over the pork.

SERVES 4

NOTE: limes and lime rind may be used in place of lemons.

PORK AND SPRING VEGETABLE STIR-FRY

100 g/4 oz broccoli or calabrese
1 tablespoon oil
2 pork steaks, cut into thin strips
100 g/4 oz cauliflower, in small florets
1 small red pepper, seeded and sliced
1 bunch spring onions, peeled, trimmed and sliced
2 teaspoons lemon juice
1 teaspoon honey

Remove the heads from the broccoli or calabrese and break into thin florets; thinly slice the stalks.

Heat the oil in a wok or frying pan, add the pork and cook for 3–4 minutes, stirring continuously, until brown. Add the broccoli or calabrese, cauliflower and red pepper and continue to cook for a further five minutes.

Stir in the remaining ingredients and stir-fry for 3 minutes more.

SERVES 2

RIGHT Pork and spring vegetable stir-fry

ROAST PORK WITH PEACH, ORANGE AND GINGER STUFFING

1.5 kg/3 lb boned loin of pork
1 onion, peeled and finely chopped
1 fresh peach, peeled, stoned and chopped
grated rind and juice of 1 orange
1 cm/½ inch piece of root ginger, peeled and
  finely chopped
50 g/2 oz fresh breadcrumbs
salt and black pepper
oil for crackling
parsley, to garnish

Preheat the oven to moderately hot (190°C, 375°F, Gas Mark 5).

Mix the onion, peach, orange rind, ginger, breadcrumbs and plenty of seasonings together. Add orange juice to bind.

Pack the stuffing into the cavity left by the bone (you may need to unroll the joint if bought ready boned and rolled), and then reroll to enclose the stuffing. Secure with string.

Brush the scored rind all over with oil and then rub with salt to ensure a good crackling.

Stand the joint in a roasting tin and cook in the preheated oven, allowing 30 minutes per 450 g/1 lb plus 30 minutes over. It is not necessary to baste during cooking, but if you add a little oil to the roasting tin, potatoes can be roasted alongside the joint for the last hour or so of cooking.

SERVES 6

BARBECUED SPARE RIBS

900 g/2 lb pork spare ribs
1 onion, peeled and finely chopped
1 garlic clove, crushed
3 tablespoons soy sauce
3 tablespoons oil
3 tablespoons cider vinegar or malt vinegar
3 tablespoons tomato purée
1 tablespoon soft brown sugar
1 teaspoon five spice powder
salt and black pepper

Put the spare rib chops in a shallow dish or tin in a single layer, if possible.

Combine the onion, garlic, soy sauce, oil, vinegar, tomato purée, sugar, five spice powder and seasonings and pour over the chops. Mix well so they are all evenly coated, cover and leave to stand for 5–6 hours, giving an occasional turn if possible.

Either cook under a moderate grill or on a well heated barbecue, allowing about 5 minutes each side or until well browned and crispy.

Alternatively, put the chops, still in the tin they were marinated in, into a fairly hot oven (200°C, 400°F, Gas Mark 6) and cook for 45–60 minutes, turning once, until cooked through and crispy.

Serve with lots of salads and new potatoes or a potato salad.

SERVES 4

BRAWN

½ pig's head
1 bouquet garni
12 black peppercorns
2 onions, peeled and sliced
2 carrots, peeled and sliced
2 sticks celery, sliced
salt and black pepper
ground nutmeg
2 teaspoons freshly chopped sage or
  1 teaspoon dried sage

Wash the head very thoroughly, making sure the ear and nostrils are very clean, then soak it in salted water for about an hour.

Cut off the ear and remove the brains. Scald the ear, scrape it free of hair and wash well.

Place the head in a large pan with the ear, bouquet garni, peppercorns and vegetables. Add 1 teaspoon salt and cover with cold water.

Bring slowly to the boil, skim and then cover and allow to cook very slowly until the meat is very tender – about 3 hours.

Strain off the liquid and reserve. Remove the meat from the bones and cut into small pieces. Skin the tongue and chop roughly. Cut the ear into strips and add to the rest of the meats.

Skim off any fat from the cooking liquid and return to a clean pan. Tie the brains in muslin and add to the pan and boil until the liquid is reduced by at least half.

Chop the brains, if liked, and add to the rest of the meat. Season the meats well with salt, pepper, nutmeg and the sage.

Pack the meat into greased cake tins or small basins and add enough of the reduced liquid to moisten. Cover each with a saucer with a weight on top. When cold, chill thoroughly.

When ready to serve: dip the container briefly into hot water and turn out on to a plate. Serve in slices.

SERVES 4

BOSTON BAKED BEANS

225 g/8 oz haricot beans, soaked overnight in cold water
450 g/1 lb lean boned belly pork, skinned
2 large onions, peeled and sliced
2 garlic cloves, peeled and crushed
1 teaspoon salt
2 teaspoons dry mustard
freshly ground black pepper
2 tablespoons black treacle
2 tablespoons vinegar
8 whole cloves
1 tablespoon tomato purée
freshly chopped parsley, to garnish

Preheat the oven to cool (150°C, 300°F, Gas Mark 2).

Drain the beans and reserve the soaking liquor. Place the beans in a large, heavy ovenproof casserole.

Trim the pork of any bones and gristle and cut into 2.5 cm/1 inch cubes. Add to the beans with the onions and just enough of the soaking liquor to cover.

Add the rest of the ingredients to the casserole and mix thoroughly.

Cover the casserole tightly and cook in the preheated oven for 6 hours.

Give the casserole a good stir and, if it looks too dry, add a little boiling water. Cover and return to the oven for a further hour.

Discard the cloves – if you can find them – and serve the casserole very hot, sprinkled with parsley and with hot crusty bread.

SERVES 4

ROAST LOIN OF PORK WITH CELERY AND APRICOT STUFFING

1.5 kg/3 lb boned and rolled loin of pork
oil
salt

Stuffing
1 tablespoon oil
1 onion, peeled and finely chopped
2 sticks celery, finely chopped
75 g/3 oz fresh white breadcrumbs
25 g/1 oz walnut halves, chopped
50 g/2 oz no-need-to-soak dried apricots, chopped
¼ teaspoon ground allspice
grated rind of ½ lemon
salt and black pepper
1 egg, beaten
celery leaves and/or parsley, to garnish

Preheat the oven to moderately hot (190°C, 375°F, Gas Mark 5).

Unroll the pork and, if necessary, cut the flesh a little so there is a pocket for the stuffing to be put in.

For the stuffing: heat the oil and fry the onion and celery for about 5 minutes or until soft. Turn into a bowl and mix in the breadcrumbs, walnuts, apricots, allspice, lemon rind and plenty of seasoning. Add the egg and bind together.

Spread the stuffing over the inside of the pork and then reroll the joint and secure with skewers and string; then remove the skewers, if possible.

Weigh the joint and calculate the cooking time, following the chart on page 28. Stand the joint in a roasting tin, rub with oil and then rub liberally with salt.

Cook as for Classic Roast Pork (see page 31) in the preheated oven for about 2 hours or 'as calculated.

Potatoes may be roasted alongside the joint for the last hour of cooking.

Serve the joint surrounded with roast potatoes, garnished with celery and/or parsley and with a gravy of pan juices.

SERVES 6

NORMANDY PORK CHOPS WITH PRUNES

4 large pork loin chops with or without kidney
salt and black pepper
225 g/8 oz no-need-to-soak stoned prunes
300 ml/½ pint apple juice
1 onion, peeled and finely chopped
1 tablespoon oil
150 ml/¼ pint stock
4 tablespoons Calvados
1 garlic clove, peeled and crushed
good pinch of ground ginger or allspice
4 tablespoons soured or fresh double cream
watercress, to garnish

Trim the chops, removing any excess fat, and season lightly.

Keep 8 prunes aside and put the remainder into a saucepan with the apple juice and onion. Bring to the boil and then simmer gently for 10 minutes until soft.

Cool slightly and then purée the prune mixture and keep aside.

Heat the oil in a large frying pan and fry the chops very gently until well browned on each side, about 10 minutes. Add the prune purée, stock, Calvados, garlic, ginger and seasonings and bring slowly to the boil. Cover and simmer for 10–15 minutes until tender.

Add the reserved prunes to the sauce and stir in the soured or fresh cream. Reheat gently and serve garnished with watercress.

SERVES 4

SOMERSET PORK

4 large boneless pork slices
2 tablespoons seasoned plain flour
1–2 tablespoons oil
175 g/6 oz button mushrooms, cleaned and trimmed
300 ml/½ pint dry cider
good dash of Worcestershire sauce
salt and black pepper
50 g/2 oz seedless raisins
1 tablespoon lemon juice
100 ml/4 fl oz single cream
freshly chopped parsley, to garnish

Trim the pork, if necessary, and coat well in seasoned flour.

Fry the chops in the heated oil until browned on both sides and almost cooked through – about 10 minutes. Remove from the pan and keep warm.

Add the mushrooms to the pan and cook gently for 2–3 minutes then stir in 1 tablespoon of the remaining seasoned flour and cook for a minute or so.

Gradually add the cider, stirring all the time, and bring up to the boil.

Add the Worcestershire sauce, plenty of seasonings, raisins and lemon juice and replace the pork.

Cover and simmer for about 10 minutes until tender. Stir in the cream, adjust the seasonings and serve sprinkled with chopped parsley.

Serve with boiled rice or pasta and a mixed green salad.

SERVES 4

SHERRIED PORK CHOPS WITH APPLE RINGS

4 pork chops
4 tablespoons dry sherry
grated rind and juice of 1 orange
2 tablespoons oil
salt and black pepper
2 medium-sized cooking apples
½ teaspoon ground cinnamon
1 tablespoon caster sugar
40 g/1½ oz butter
watercress, to garnish

Place the pork chops in a dish in a single layer. Combine the sherry, orange rind and juice and oil and season well. Pour over the chops, cover and leave in a cool place to marinate for at least 4 hours and preferably overnight.

When ready to cook: peel and core the apples and cut into thick slices. Put on a plate and sprinkle with cinnamon and sugar. Melt the butter, pour over the apple rings and turn so they are evenly coated.

Cook the apple rings under a moderate grill for about 2 minutes each side, then transfer to a serving dish and keep warm.

Lift the pork chops out of the marinade and cook under the preheated grill, allowing 8–10 minutes each side, until cooked through.

Serve the chops topped with apple slices and garnished with watercress with sauté potatoes and a green vegetable or salad.

SERVES 4

PIZZA QUICKIE

225 g/8 oz wholewheat flour
salt and black pepper
50 g/2 oz margarine
2 eggs, beaten
2 tablespoons milk
1 onion, peeled and chopped
100 g/4 oz mushrooms, sliced
1 tablespoon oil
1 × 400 g/14 oz can peeled tomatoes, drained
350 g/12 oz cooked ham, chopped
1 teaspoon mixed herbs
100 g/4 oz mature Cheddar cheese, grated

Preheat the oven to very hot (230°C, 450°F, Gas Mark 8).

Put the flour into a bowl with a good pinch of salt and rub in the margarine until the mixture resembles fine breadcrumbs.

Add the eggs and milk to form a softish dough, knead lightly and divide the mixture into four portions.

Roll out each piece of dough to a 15 cm/6 inch round and place on greased baking sheets.

Fry the onion and mushrooms in the oil until soft for about 5 minutes. Stir in the tomatoes and ham and season well.

Spread over each pizza base to cover and then sprinkle first with herbs and then with cheese.

Bake in the preheated very hot oven for 12–15 minutes and serve hot with a salad.

SERVES 4

PORK TIKKA

450 g/1 lb lean pork, cubed
8 button mushrooms, trimmed
½ red pepper, cut into 8 pieces
oil for brushing

Marinade
150 ml/¼ pint plain, unsweetened yogurt
2.5 cm/1 inch piece root ginger, peeled and
*   finely grated*
1 garlic clove, crushed
½ teaspoon paprika
salt and black pepper
red liquid food colouring (optional)

Mix together all the ingredients for the marinade, adding a few drops of red colouring if liked.

Add the pork to the marinade, toss well, cover and leave in a cool place for at least 3 hours and preferably overnight.

When ready to cook, thread the pork onto 4 long skewers alternating with the mushrooms and pieces of pepper. Brush with oil.

Cook under a moderately heated grill or on a barbecue for 12–14 minutes, turning several times and brushing with the marinade at least once during cooking.

Serve with freshly boiled rice and coleslaw.

SERVES 4

PORK AND APPLE BURGERS

450 g/1 lb minced pork
1 cooking apple, peeled, cored and coarsely
*   grated*
1 bunch spring onions, trimmed and
*   chopped*
grated rind of 1 lemon
salt and black pepper

Mix together all the ingredients, adding plenty of salt and pepper.

Divide into 4 or 8 equal portions and shape each one into a burger shape.

Put on to a grill rack and cook under a moderate grill for about 5–7 minutes each side until well browned and cooked.

Serve with a mixed salad.

SERVES 4

Pork tikka

PORK AND CELERY CASSEROLE

450 g/1 lb lean pork, cubed
1 onion, peeled and sliced
2 garlic cloves, crushed
1 tablespoon oil
100 g/4 oz mushrooms
1 beef stock cube
600 ml/1 pint dry cider
1 teaspoon dried sweet basil
2 bay leaves
salt and black pepper
1 tablespoon cornflour
100 g/4 oz frozen or canned sweetcorn
175 g/6 oz celery, sliced
freshly chopped parsley, to garnish

Preheat the oven to moderate (160°C, 325°F, Gas Mark 3).

Fry the pork, onion and garlic in the oil until well sealed and the onions are lightly browned. Add the mushrooms and continue cooking for 2 minutes.

Crumble the stock cube into the cider and add to the pan with the basil, bay leaves and plenty of seasonings.

Transfer to a casserole, cover and cook in the preheated oven for 1½ hours.

Blend the cornflour with 2 tablespoons water and stir into the casserole with the sweetcorn and celery. Recover and return to the oven for 30 minutes.

Serve the casserole garnished with chopped parsley and with noodles or baked jacket potatoes.

SERVES 4

RAISED PORK PIE

750 g /1½ lb lean pork
1 dessert apple, peeled and cored
1 large onion, peeled
1 garlic clove, peeled and crushed
salt and black pepper
good pinch each of sage and thyme

Hot water crust pastry
450 g/1 lb plain flour
1 teaspoon salt
100 g/4 oz lard
200 ml/7 fl oz milk and water mixed
beaten egg, to glaze
2 teaspoons powdered gelatine
250 ml/8 fl oz stock

Mince half the pork with the apple and onion and put into a bowl. Add the garlic, seasonings and sage and thyme.

Finely chop the remainder of the pork and mix evenly through the minced meat.

For the pastry: sift the flour and salt into a bowl and make a well in the centre. Put the lard and water into a pan, heat until the fat dissolves and then bring up to the boil.

Pour the liquid all at once into the well in the flour and mix quickly to form a fairly soft dough. Turn on to a lightly floured surface and knead lightly until smooth. Remove three-quarters of it and keep the remainder in a bowl covered with a cloth.

Roll out the pastry and use to line a lightly greased round cake tin of 18–20 cm/7–8 inches in diameter and preferably with a loose base.

Put the pork mixture into the pastry case, making sure it is evenly packed.

Roll out the reserved pastry and use for a lid. Damp the edges, position and press the edges well together. Trim off surplus pastry and crimp.

Use the pastry trimmings to make leaves to decorate the top of the pie. Make a hole in the centre of the lid for steam to escape.

Stand the pie on a baking sheet and glaze with beaten egg. Cook in a preheated fairly hot oven (200°C, 400°F, Gas Mark 6) for 30

minutes. Reduce the oven to moderate (160°C, 325°F, Gas Mark 3), glaze the pie again and cook for a further 1¼–1½ hours. If it tends to overbrown, lay a sheet of greaseproof paper over the top.

Dissolve the gelatine in the stock and season well. As the pie begins to cool, pour the stock into the pie through a small funnel inserted into the central hole. Fill up at intervals until full.

When the pie is cold, chill thoroughly at least overnight, before turning out.

SERVES 8–10

NOTE: if you like, 4 small hard-boiled eggs may be embedded in the pork mixture as it is packed into the pastry case.

CHINESE PORK STIR-FRY

450 g/1 lb boneless leg of pork, cut into narrow strips
2 garlic cloves, crushed
1 tablespoon oil
1 large onion, peeled and thinly sliced
100 g/4 oz mushrooms, sliced
100 g/4 oz green pepper, cut into thin strips
1 × 350 g/12 oz can pineapple cubes in natural juice
1 × 200 g/7 oz can water chestnuts, drained and sliced
300 g/10 oz bean sprouts
salt and black pepper
3 tablespoons soy sauce
2 tablespoons sherry
1 teaspoon ground cumin

Fry the pork and garlic in the oil for about 5 minutes, preferably in a Chinese wok, or a large frying pan.

Add the onion and fry for 2 minutes.

Add all the rest of the ingredients, mix well and cook for a further 7–8 minutes, stirring frequently.

Serve at once with fried rice or noodles.

SERVES 4

PORK FILLET IN A CRUST

450 g/1 lb pork tenderloin or fillet
2 teaspoons oil

Stuffing
2 teaspoons oil
1 small onion, peeled and finely chopped
4 lean rashers of bacon, derinded and
*   chopped*
1 medium cooking apple, peeled, cored and
*   coarsely grated or finely chopped*
75 g/3 oz mushrooms, chopped
¼ teaspoon dried thyme
grated rind of ½ orange
salt and black pepper

350 g/12 oz ready-made puff pastry
beaten egg, to glaze
watercress or herbs, to garnish

Sauce
1 tablespoon plain flour
4 tablespoons wine (red or white) or cider
2 tablespoons orange juice
275 ml/scant ½ pint stock
1 tablespoon tomato purée

Cut the pork fillets to about 23 cm/9 inches long to make an even-sized joint, then tie together with fine string into a neat shape.

Heat the oil in a pan and fry the pork very gently for about 15 minutes, turning it regularly until evenly browned all over. Remove from the pan and allow to cool.

Stir the flour for the sauce into the pan juices and cook for a minute or so. Gradually add the wine or cider, orange juice, stock and tomato purée. Bring up to the boil and simmer for 2–3 minutes. Leave to cool.

For the stuffing: heat a little oil in a pan and fry the onion and bacon gently until soft. Add the apple and mushrooms and continue for a minute or so. Remove from the heat, stir in the thyme, orange rind and seasonings and leave to cool.

Now preheat the oven to hot (220°C, 425°F, Gas Mark 7).

Roll out the pastry, large enough to

enclose the pork joint. Spread the stuffing down the centre of the pastry.

Remove the string from the pork and stand it on top of the stuffing.

Wrap the pastry around the pork to completely enclose it, sealing the edges with water or beaten egg. Stand in a lightly greased roasting tin with the pastry joins underneath.

Decorate the top with leaves cut from the pastry trimmings and glaze overall very thoroughly with beaten egg.

Make one or two holes in the pastry for steam to escape, put in the preheated oven and cook for 30 minutes.

Reduce the temperature to moderate (180°C, 350°F, Gas Mark 4) and continue for about 20–25 minutes until the pastry is well puffed up and golden brown. If it overbrowns, lay a sheet of greaseproof paper over it.

Reheat the sauce, strain into a jug and serve with the pork, which should be cut into fairly thick slices and garnished with watercress or herbs.

SERVES 4–5

CRISPY TOPPED PORK CASSOULET

2 tablespoons oil
750 g/1½ lb lean pork, cut into 2.5 cm/1
*   inch cubes*
1 large onion, peeled and finely chopped
4 sticks celery, thinly sliced
1 large red or orange pepper, deseeded and
*   sliced*
2 garlic cloves, peeled and crushed
4 tablespoons medium sherry
2 tablespoons soy sauce
2 tablespoons lemon juice
300 ml/½ pint stock
salt and black pepper
1 × 425 g/15 oz can red kidney beans

Topping
50 g/2 oz butter or margarine
40 g/1½ oz fresh breadcrumbs
40 g/1½ oz blanched almonds, chopped
freshly chopped parsley, to garnish

Preheat the oven to moderate (180°C, 350°F, Gas Mark 4).

Heat the oil in a pan and fry the pieces of pork until browned all over. Transfer to a casserole.

Add the onion, celery, pepper and garlic to the pan and fry for 2–3 minutes, stirring continuously, then add to the casserole.

Add the sherry, soy sauce, lemon juice and stock to the pan and bring up to the boil. Season well and add the drained beans. Pour into the casserole and mix well.

Cover tightly and cook in a moderate oven for 50–60 minutes until tender.

Just before the cassoulet is ready, melt the butter for the topping in a frying pan. Add the breadcrumbs and fry gently, stirring all the time until beginning to brown. Add the almonds and continue until both crumbs and nuts are golden brown.

To serve: remove the lid from the cassoulet, spoon off any excess fat from the surface and give a good stir. Spoon the crispy topping evenly over it and sprinkle with parsley.

SERVES 5–6

TARRAGON PORK SALAD

350 g/12 oz pork tenderloin cut into 1 cm/¼
  inch slices
4 tablespoons oil
2 tablespoons orange juice
2 tablespoons chopped fresh tarragon
salt and black pepper

Salad
225 g/8 oz small new potatoes, boiled and
  cooled
100 g/4 oz French beans, blanched
6 cherry tomatoes, halved
3 tablespoons oil
1 tablespoon orange juice
1 teaspoon honey
2 teaspoons chopped fresh tarragon
salt and black pepper

Lay the pork in a shallow dish. Mix the oil, orange juice, tarragon and seasonings together and pour over the pork. Cover and marinate in a cool place for 3–4 hours.

Remove the pork from the marinade, reserving the marinade. Barbecue or grill the pork until cooked, turning it once and brushing with the marinade.

Mix the potatoes, French beans and tomatoes together.

Put the remaining ingredients in a screw-top jar and shake well to make a dressing. Pour the dressing over the potato salad.

To serve, arrange the pork slices round the edge of a serving plate and put the salad in the centre.

SERVES 2

BACON CHOPS WITH PLUM SAUCE

4 back bacon chops, about 2.5 cm/1 inch thick, rinds removed
175 g/6 oz plum jam
4 tablespoons wine vinegar
4 tablespoons water
2 teaspoons dry mustard
freshly ground black pepper
large pinch of mixed herbs
¼ teaspoon ground cinnamon
½ teaspoon cornflour
watercress, to garnish

Cut deep slashes into the fat of the bacon chops at about 2 cm/¾ inch intervals to prevent curling up during cooking.

Put the jam into a saucepan with the vinegar, water, mustard, pepper, herbs and cinnamon. Heat gently until quite disolved and then simmer for 2–3 minutes. If liked, blend the cornflour with a little cold water and add to the sauce and bring back to the boil.

Stand the chops on a grill rack and cook under a moderate grill for 4–5 minutes each side. Turn over when the fat is brown and crispy.

Serve the chops with sauce spooned over and garnished with watercress. Creamed potatoes and spinach make good accompaniments.

SERVES 4

BACON AND ONION FLAN

Pastry
175 g/6 oz granary flour
salt
40 g/1½ oz butter or margarine
40 g/1½ oz lard or white fat
about 2 tablespoons cold water to mix

Filling
1 tablespoon oil
350 g/12 oz onions, peeled and thinly sliced
175 g/6 oz streaky bacon rashers, derinded
2 eggs
300 ml/½ pint single cream
salt and black pepper
50 g/2 oz Gruyère cheese, grated
12 stuffed olives, halved

For the pastry: put the flour into a bowl with a pinch of salt and rub in the fats until the mixture resembles fine breadcrumbs.

Add sufficient water to mix to a pliable dough, knead lightly until smooth, then wrap in a polythene bag and chill whilst preparing the filling.

Heat the oil in a pan and fry the onions very gently for 10–15 minutes until very soft and lightly browned, stirring from time to time. Drain thoroughly and cool.

Grill or fry the bacon in its own fat until crispy, drain well and then crumble or chop.

Roll out the pastry and use to line a 20 cm/8 inch flan ring, tin or dish. Spread the onions in the base and sprinkle with the bacon.

Beat the eggs with the cream and a pinch of salt and plenty of black pepper and pour over the bacon. Sprinkle evenly with the grated cheese. Arrange the olives cut side upwards over the surface of the flan.

Cook in a preheated hot oven (200°C, 400°F, Gas Mark 6) for about 40 minutes until the filling is set and golden brown and the pastry cooked through. Serve the flan hot or cold.

SERVES 4–6

INDONESIA PORK RISOTTO

2 tablespoons oil
2 onions, peeled and sliced
1 garlic clove, peeled and crushed
2 carrots, peeled and diced
2 sticks celery, sliced
2 teaspoons curry powder
1 tablespoon soy sauce
½ teaspoon ground coriander
salt and black pepper
350 g/12 oz cooked pork, cut into narrow strips
175 g/6 oz long grain rice, freshly boiled
175 g/6 oz peas, freshly cooked
2 eggs
15 g/½ oz butter or margarine

Heat the oil in a large pan and fry the onions, garlic, carrots and celery gently for about 10 minutes, until soft but only lightly coloured.

Add the curry powder, soy sauce, coriander and seasonings and mix well.

Add the cooked pork and cook in the mixture, stirring continuously for about 5 minutes, until well cooked through.

Add the well drained rice and peas and mix evenly through the pan. Turn on to a serving dish and keep warm.

Beat the eggs with salt and pepper and 1 tablespoon water. Melt the fat in a frying pan and when hot, pour in the beaten eggs. Cook undisturbed until set. Turn on to a plate and cut into narrow strips. Arrange these over the risotto and serve.

SERVES 4

LEFT Tarragon pork salad

POT ROAST COLLAR BACON

1 × 1.5 kg/3 lb prime collar joint of bacon
20 whole cloves
20 button onions, peeled
1 tablespoon oil
2 garlic cloves, peeled and crushed
450 g/1 lb tomatoes, peeled and quartered
1 teaspoon dried sage
300 ml/½ pint dry cider
2 tablespoons dry breadcrumbs (optional)
2 teaspoons cornflour
chopped parsley, to garnish

Soak the bacon joint in cold water for 6–12 hours if a smoked joint.

Put into a saucepan with clean water, bring to the boil, remove the scum, cover and simmer for 45 minutes.

Drain the bacon, strip off the skin and stand in a casserole. Score the fat and stud with cloves.

Fry the onions in the oil until lightly browned and then arrange around the bacon joint, with the garlic, tomatoes, and sage.

Bring the cider to the boil, pour over the bacon, cover the casserole and cook in a moderately hot oven (190°C, 375°F, Gas Mark 5) for an hour.

Remove the lid from the casserole, and, if liked, sprinkle the bacon fat with dry breadcrumbs. Return to the oven, uncovered, for 10–15 minutes until lightly browned.

Remove the bacon joint, tomatoes and onions to a serving dish. Skim off any fat from the cooking juices and thicken with 1–2 teaspoons cornflour blended in a little cold water. Bring back to the boil, season to taste and serve with the bacon, which has been garnished with chopped parsley.

SERVES 6

BACON AND SPINACH SALAD

225 g/8 oz fresh spinach leaves
350 g/12 oz streaky or back bacon rashers, derinded
6–8 spring onions, trimmed and sliced
2 dessert apples, cored and chopped
2 tablespoons French dressing
4–6 hard-boiled eggs, quartered
50 g/2 oz blanched almonds, cut into strips and toasted
6 tablespoons mayonnaise
cherry tomatoes

Strip the stalks from the spinach, then wash and dry thoroughly. Tear up roughly and put into a bowl.

Either grill the bacon or fry in its own fat until crispy and drain very well. When cold either crumble or chop.

Add the bacon to the spinach with the onions.

Toss the apples in the French dressing and add it all to the spinach and toss well.

Turn the salad on to a platter and arrange the quartered hard-boiled eggs in the centre. Spoon the mayonnaise over the eggs and then sprinkle with the almonds.

Arrange cherry tomatoes (or wedges of larger tomatoes if unavailable) around the edge of the salad and serve.

SERVES 4

SUGAR-GLAZED GAMMON

1 × 1.5–1.75 kg/3–4 lb gammon joint
6 whole cloves
2 bay leaves
1 onion, peeled and sliced
100 g/4 oz demerara sugar
2 tablespoons wine vinegar
1 tablespoon honey

Glazed apples
2–3 dessert apples
25 g/1 oz butter, melted
ground cinnamon
watercress, to garnish

Weigh the joint and calculate the cooking time, allowing 25 minutes per 450 g/1 lb plus 25 minutes over. Place in a large saucepan, add the cloves, bay leaves, onion, 25 g/1 oz sugar and water to cover.

Bring up to the boil, remove any scum, cover and simmer gently for half of the total cooking time.

Preheat the oven to moderate (180°C, 350°F, Gas Mark 4).

Drain the joint, stand on a sheet of foil and package. Stand in a roasting tin and cook in the preheated oven until 30 minutes before the end of cooking time.

Fold back the foil, strip off the skin and score the fat into diamonds. Heat the vinegar and honey together and brush liberally over the fat. Sprinkle evenly with the remaining sugar, pressing it in.

Return to the oven for the rest of the cooking time until the topping is crisp and browning.

Meanwhile, peel the apples and cut out the central core with an apple corer. Slice. Stand on a foil-lined grill rack and brush with melted butter. Sprinkle lightly with cinnamon and cook under a moderate grill until lightly browned.

Serve the gammon surrounded with apple slices and garnished with watercress.

To serve cold, simply leave the joint until cold and then chill and serve in slices.

SERVES 8

OFFAL

LIVER MARSALA

450 g/1 lb lambs' liver, sliced
little seasoned plain flour
40 g/1½ oz butter
8 rashers streaky bacon, derinded
4–6 tablespoons Marsala
150 ml/¼ pint beef stock
1–2 tablespoons lemon juice
little grated lemon rind
salt and black pepper
1 tablespoon freshly chopped parsley
1½ teaspoons freshly chopped thyme
sprigs of fresh herbs, to garnish

Trim the liver and coat all over in seasoned flour.

Melt the butter in a large frying pan. Cut each rasher of bacon into 3 or 4 pieces and fry gently in the fat until lightly coloured, then remove from the pan.

Fry the slices of liver in the same pan until browned on both sides. Add the marsala, stock and 1 tablespoon lemon juice and rind and bring to the boil. Season well and replace the bacon.

Cover the pan and simmer gently for about 15 minutes until the liver is tender. Adjust the seasonings, sharpen with lemon juice, if necessary, and stir in the chopped herbs. Serve garnished with sprigs of fresh herbs and with fried or new potatoes and a salad.

NOTE: a spoonful of plain, unsweetened yogurt can be added to each portion for a change.

LAMB'S LIVER WITH APPLES AND PEARS

450 g/1 lb lamb's liver, sliced
25 g/1 oz plain flour, seasoned with salt and pepper
1 tablespoon oil
1 garlic clove, peeled and crushed
1 eating apple, cored and sliced
1 pear, cored and sliced
1 teaspoon fresh sage, chopped
150 ml/¼ pint apple juice
sprigs fresh sage, to garnish

Coat the liver in the seasoned flour. Heat the oil in a frying pan and brown the liver on both sides.

Remove the liver from the pan, add the garlic, apple and pear and cook for 2 minutes. Add the sage and apple juice and bring to the boil.

Return the liver to the pan and simmer, covered, for 15 minutes.

Serve the liver garnished with sprigs of fresh sage.

SERVES 4

TRIPE AND TOMATO STEW

675–900 g/1½–2 lb dressed tripe
600 ml/1 pint milk
600 ml/1 pint water
3–4 tablespoons olive or other oil
2 large onions, peeled and sliced
1 garlic clove, crushed
100 g/4 oz mushrooms, trimmed and halved if large
450 g/1 lb tomatoes, peeled and chopped
1 bay leaf
1 tablespoon freshly chopped parsley
pinch of dried rosemary
pinch of grated nutmeg
150 ml/¼ pint dry cider
300 ml/½ pint beef stock
salt and black pepper

Wash the tripe and place in a large saucepan with the milk and water. Bring up to the boil, cover and cook until tender, for 45–50 minutes.

Drain the tripe and cut into strips.

Heat the oil in a pan and fry the onions and garlic until soft and lightly browned, then add the mushrooms and tripe and fry for 3–4 minutes, stirring frequently.

Add the tomatoes, herbs and spices, cider and 150 ml/¼ pint stock. Season well and bring up to the boil. Cover and simmer for 1–1½ hours until the tripe is very tender, adding more stock if necessary during cooking.

Serve very hot with boiled or creamed potatoes and a green vegetable.

SERVES 4–6

KIDNEYS TURBIGO

2 tablespoons oil
8 lambs' kidneys, skinned, cored and halved
350 g/12 oz pork chipolata sausages,
    twisted in half
12–16 button onions, peeled
225 g/8 oz button mushrooms, trimmed
4 teaspoons plain flour
275 ml/scant ½ pint beef stock
4 tablespoons dry sherry
salt and black pepper
chopped parsley, to garnish

Heat the oil in a frying pan and fry the kidneys to seal, then remove from the pan.

Add the chipolatas to the pan and fry until browned all over; then remove from the pan.

Fry the onions until golden brown in the same pan, then add the mushrooms and continue for a minute or so.

Stir in the flour and cook for one minute, then gradually add the stock, stirring until it boils and thickens. Add the sherry and seasonings and return the kidneys and chipolatas to the pan.

Cover the pan and simmer gently for 20–25 minutes until tender. Adjust the seasonings and serve liberally sprinkled with chopped parsley and with freshly cooked pasta or rice.

SERVES 4

LIVER AND ORANGE
(*MICROWAVE RECIPE*)

225 g/8 oz lambs' liver, sliced
15 g/½ oz butter
1 medium onion, peeled and thinly sliced
1 garlic clove, peeled and crushed
2 medium oranges
salt and black pepper
watercress, to garnish

Heat the browning dish for 6 (7) minutes. Put the butter, onion and garlic in the dish and cook on High (100%) for 1 (2) minutes.

Press the slices of liver on to the dish and cook on High (100%) for 1 (2) minutes. Turn the liver over and cook for a further 1 (2) minutes.

Squeeze the juice from one orange, add seasonings and pour over the liver. Cook on High (100%) for 4 (6) minutes.

Remove the peel and pith from the second orange and cut out the segments free of membrane. Add to the liver during the last minute of the cooking time. Serve garnished with watercress and with green vegetables or a salad.

SERVES 2

NOTE: instructions are for a 650-watt oven, with figures for 500-watt oven given in brackets.

ITALIAN-STYLE KIDNEYS

175 g/6 oz button mushrooms, trimmed
    and quartered
2 tablespoons chopped parsley
1–2 garlic cloves, crushed
1 tablespoon chopped chives or sliced spring
    onions
4 tomatoes, peeled, quartered and seeded
10 lambs' kidneys, skinned, halved and
    cored
little seasoned plain flour
40 g/1½ oz butter
2 tablespoons oil
salt and black pepper
2 tablespoons lemon juice

Put the mushrooms into a bowl with the parsley, garlic, chives or onions and tomatoes and mix together.

Coat the kidneys in seasoned flour. Melt the butter and oil in a frying pan and fry the kidneys for 3–4 minutes until well sealed and just cooked.

Lift the kidneys from the pan and keep warm.

Add the mushroom mixture to the pan and cook gently for 3–4 minutes, stirring carefully so the tomatoes do not break up too much. Season very well and add the lemon juice.

Return the kidneys to the pan and reheat thoroughly without over-cooking. Serve with freshly boiled rice.

SERVES 4

LIVER WITH APPLES AND DILL

450 g/1 lb lambs' liver, sliced
2 tablespoons seasoned plain flour
25 g/1 oz butter
1 tablespoon oil
350 g/12 oz cooking apples, peeled, cored
    and sliced
1 tablespoon freshly chopped parsley
1 teaspoon freshly chopped thyme
1 tablespoon freshly chopped dill
300 ml/½ pint beef stock
salt and black pepper
fresh dill, to garnish

Coat the slices of liver evenly in seasoned flour.

Melt the butter and oil in a frying pan and fry the liver for 2–3 minutes each side until well sealed; then remove from the pan.

Add the apples to the pan and fry gently for 4–5 minutes, taking care not to break up the slices. Sprinkle in the herbs and add the stock.

Bring up to the boil, season well and carefully replace the liver. Cover the pan and simmer gently for 10–15 minutes until tender. Taste and adjust the seasoning.

Serve very hot, garnished with sprigs of fresh dill and with creamed potatoes and a salad.

SERVES 4

RIGHT Kidneys turbigo

TRIPE AND ONIONS

*750 g/1½ lb dressed tripe, blanket or
   honeycomb or a mixture*
600 ml/1 pint milk
salt and black pepper
1 bay leaf (preferably fresh)
*450 g/1 lb onions, peeled and quartered or
   roughly chopped*
25 g/1 oz butter
25 g/1 oz plain flour
1 tablespoon freshly chopped parsley
*1 teaspoon freshly chopped thyme
   (optional)*

Cut the dressed tripe into 4 cm/1½ inch
cubes and put into a saucepan. Cover with
cold water, bring up to the boil and simmer
for 5 minutes. Drain.

Put the drained tripe back into the
saucepan with the milk, seasonings and
bay leaf. Bring to the boil and cover the pan.
Simmer very gently for an hour.

Add the onions and continue to simmer
gently for 45 minutes.

Strain off the cooking liquor and make up
to 450 ml/¾ pint with more milk or water, if
necessary.

Melt the butter in a pan, stir in the flour
and cook for a minute or so then gradually
add the cooking liquor and bring up to the
boil, stirring continuously. Return the tripe
to the sauce, discarding the bay leaf, and
reheat until piping hot.

Adjust the seasonings and stir in the
herbs, or alternatively sprinkle the herbs
over the tripe. Serve with mashed potatoes
and carrots.

SERVES 4

KIDNEY FRITTERS WITH MUSTARD DIP

*150 ml/¼ pint plain, unsweetened yogurt or
   soured cream*
*1 tablespoon coarse-grain tarragon-
   flavoured mustard*
1 garlic clove, peeled and crushed
salt and black pepper
*10–12 lambs' kidneys, skinned, halved and
   cored*
little seasoned plain flour
100 g/4 oz plain flour
1 large egg
125 ml/scant ¼ pint milk
1 teaspoon oil
oil for deep frying

To garnish
mustard and cress
cherry tomatoes

First make the sauce by combining the
yogurt or soured cream with the mustard,
garlic and plenty of seasonings to taste.
Turn into a bowl and cover until required.

Toss the kidney halves in seasoned flour.

Sift the flour into a bowl with a pinch of
salt for the batter. Add the egg and sufficient milk to mix to a smooth and fairly
thick batter, then beat in the oil and
remaining milk.

Heat the oil to 180–190°C/350–375°F, or
until a cube of bread browns in about 30
seconds.

Toss the kidneys in seasoned flour again
and then dip them, a few at a time, into the
batter. Drop into the hot oil and fry for 3–4
minutes until golden brown and crisp.
Drain the fritters on absorbent kitchen
paper and keep warm whilst frying the
remainder.

Serve hot, garnished with mustard and
cress and cherry tomatoes (or wedges of
tomato) and with the dip.

SERVES 4

PRESSED TONGUE

*1 salted or pickled ox tongue, approx.
   1.5 kg/3½ lb*
*2 onions, peeled and each studded with 4
   cloves*
2 bay leaves (preferably fresh)
2 carrots, peeled and sliced
2 sticks celery, sliced
salads, to garnish

Soak the tongue in cold water for 12–24
hours if you do not want it to be too salty
when cooked. Drain the tongue and place in
a saucepan of clean cold water. Add the
onions, bay leaves, carrots and celery and
bring up to the boil.

Remove any scum from the surface,
cover the pan and simmer gently for about
3½ hours, adding more boiling water as
necessary, until the tongue is tender when
checked with a fine skewer.

Drain the tongue and immediately
plunge it into cold water. Remove the skin
and any bones and gristle from the thick
end of the tongue.

Put the tongue on to a board and cut in
half lengthwise with a sharp knife. Place
one half, cut side downwards, in a round 15
cm/6 inch cake tin, curling it round to fit it.

Arrange the second half of the tongue
with the cut side upwards on top of the first
piece. Cover with a saucer and put a heavy
weight on the saucer. Leave until quite cold
and then chill at least overnight and preferably for a little longer.

Turn the tongue out carefully on to a
serving dish and garnish with salads. Serve
cut into thin slices.

SERVES 8–10

NOTE: to serve the tongue hot, remove the
skin as above and then place the hot tongue
in one piece on a serving dish. A marsala or
port sauce makes a good accompaniment.

BRAISED HEARTS IN WINE SAUCE

2 large onions, peeled and chopped
1 tablespoon oil
100 g/4 oz fresh white breadcrumbs
2 teaspoons dried sage
salt and black pepper
4 lambs' hearts
1 large onion, peeled and thinly sliced
2 tablespoons oil
300 ml/½ pint beef stock
150 ml/¼ pint red wine
2 teaspoons cornflour
chopped parsley, to garnish

Preheat the oven to moderate (180°C, 350°F, Gas Mark 4).

For the stuffing: put the onions into a pan of cold water, bring to the boil and simmer for 10 minutes, then drain very thoroughly.

Heat the oil in a pan and fry the onions for 2–3 minutes, without colouring.

Put the breadcrumbs, sage and seasonings into a bowl, add the onions and the fat and mix together.

Trim the hearts, making sure all the tubes and arteries have been removed. Use the stuffing to fill the cavities of the hearts and sew together loosely with thread.

Heat the oil in a pan and fry the hearts until well browned all over. Transfer to a casserole. Fry the sliced onion in the same fat until golden brown.

Add the stock and wine to the pan and bring up to the boil. Season well and pour over the hearts in the casserole. Cover the casserole tightly.

Cook in the preheated oven for 1½ hours or until very tender. Blend the cornflour with a little cold water and stir evenly through the casserole. Return to the oven for 5 minutes to thicken.

Remove the threads from the hearts, adjust the seasonings to the sauce and serve sprinkled with chopped parsley and with creamed potatoes and a green vegetable.

SERVES 4

BRAISED OX HEART WITH ORANGE

900 g/2 lb ox heart
2 tablespoons oil
2 large onions, peeled and sliced
1 garlic clove, peeled and crushed
3 tablespoons plain flour
300 ml/½ pint beef stock
150 ml/¼ pint white wine
finely grated rind of 1 orange
juice of 2 oranges
salt and black pepper
2 tablespoons orange marmalade
1–2 oranges, peeled and cut into segments
    free of membrane
675 g/1½ lb creamed potato

To garnish
julienne strips of orange rind, blanched
parsley sprigs

Preheat the oven to cool (150°C, 300°F, Gas Mark 2).

Cut the heart into narrow strips, removing any tubes and gristle, then wash very thoroughly and dry.

Heat the oil in a pan and fry the strips of heart until lightly browned and transfer to a casserole. Add the onions and garlic to the pan and fry until lightly browned.

Stir in the flour and cook for a minute or so and then gradually add the stock and wine and bring up to the boil. Stir in the orange rind, orange juice, and marmalade and season well. Pour into the casserole and cover tightly.

Cook in a cool oven for about 2¾ hours or until tender, checking after 2 hours to see if a little more stock should be added. Add the orange segments and return to the oven for 5–10 minutes.

Meanwhile, pipe the creamed potato around the edge of the shallow fireproof dish and brown under a moderate grill.

Spoon the heart mixture into the centre of the potato and sprinkle with the julienne strips of orange rind and garnish with parsley sprigs.

SERVES 4

NOTE: for julienne strips of orange rind, first pare the rind from a firm orange with a potato peeler and then cut into very narrow strips. Cook in boiling water for 5 minutes until tender, drain and use.

CRISPY FRIED BRAINS

450 g/1 lb calves' or lambs' brains
1 onion, peeled and chopped
salt and black pepper
3 tablespoons vinegar
little seasoned flour
1–2 eggs, beaten
75 g/3 oz fresh white breadcrumbs
oil for shallow frying
lemon wedges, to garnish

Soak the brains in cold water for 1–2 hours then rinse under cold running water and drain thoroughly. Remove any arteries and membranes with a sharp knife and make sure all traces of blood have been removed.

Put the brains in a saucepan and add the onion, plenty of seasonings, the vinegar and cold water to cover. Bring to the boil, very slowly, and then cover the pan and simmer gently for 5 minutes.

Drain the brains and plunge into a bowl of cold water, then when cold, drain well.

Cut the brains into smaller pieces, if preferred, and roll in seasoned flour. Dip in beaten egg and then roll in breadcrumbs until thoroughly coated.

Fry in well-heated shallow oil until a pale golden brown all over and crispy. Drain on absorbent paper and keep warm whilst frying the remainder.

Serve hot garnished with lemon wedges and with tartare sauce. If liked, they may be lightly dusted with paprika before serving.
SERVES 4

BOAR'S HEAD

1 pig's head
75 g/3 oz powdered gelatine (6 sachets)
450 ml/¾ pint beef stock
about 175 g/6 oz lard or white fat
1 green dessert apple (not too big)
gravy browning (optional)
2 glass teddy bear's eyes

To garnish
parsley sprigs
evergreen leaves
salads

This dish is usually only prepared for display, not to be eaten; however, once the display is over, provided the head is still fresh it can be stripped of the glaze, re-boiled for about 1½ hours and made into brawn.

Open the pig's mouth and hold open with a piece of wood or something solid. Place in a very large saucepan, supporting the ears with foil, bending them inwards if necessary to fit in the pan.

Cover with water and a lid and bring slowly to the boil. Simmer very gently for 3 hours. Remove from the heat and allow to cool overnight.

The next day, drain off all the water, remove the wood from the mouth and chill the head very thoroughly and then probably for about 1 hour in the freezer just before adding the glaze.

For the glaze: add the gelatine to 150 ml/¼ pint of the stock and allow to stand for 5–10 minutes until it becomes really spongy. Add the remaining stock and put into a saucepan and heat gently until really dissolved. If it seems a very pale colour, add a little gravy browning, for the glaze should be quite dark brown. Allow to cool but not set.

Make sure the pig's head is smooth and free from loose pieces of skin. Using a pastry brush, brush all over with the glaze which should set as it touches the cold head. Return to the refrigerator for about an hour.

Melt the remaining glaze down and add a second coat to the head. Chill.

Carefully place the apple in the mouth and position the eyes, leaving them sticking out a little on their wires.

Soften the lard or white fat until of a piping consistency. Put into a piping bag fitted with a large star nozzle and decorate the head. First outline each eye and ear, then outline the nose and mouth and add fancy shapes to the cheeks and head.

Stand the head carefully on a board or large dish and surround with evergreen leaves, parsley and salads.

LIVER AND POTATO PAN BAKE

1 tablespoon oil
2 large onions, peeled and sliced
450 g/1 lb potatoes, thinly sliced
salt and black pepper
75 g/3 oz sweetcorn kernels
225 g/8 oz lamb's liver, cut into strips
4 rashers rindless streaky smoked bacon, chopped
150 ml/¼ pint plain unsweetened yogurt
paprika

Put the oil in a large frying pan. Layer the onions and potatoes in the pan, seasoning them well. Sprinkle over the sweetcorn. Arrange the liver and bacon on top.

Cover the pan with a close-fitting lid or kitchen foil and cook on a low heat for 30 minutes, or until the potatoes are tender.

Pour the yogurt over and sprinkle over the paprika before serving.
SERVES 2

RIGHT Liver and potato pan bake

BRAINS A L'ANGLAISE

4 sets lambs' brains
600 ml/1 pint beef stock
2 tablespoons vinegar
2 onions, peeled and finely chopped
50 g/2 oz butter
4 tablespoons white wine
salt and black pepper
4 slices toast
paprika and chopped parsley, to garnish

Soak the brains in cold water for 1–2 hours to remove all traces of blood. Rinse under cold running water and drain thoroughly. Remove any arteries and membranes with a sharp knife.

Place in a saucepan with the stock and vinegar and bring up to the boil. Cover and simmer for 10–15 minutes, depending on size. Drain and plunge into a bowl of cold water and when cold drain again.

Fry the onions in the melted butter very gently until soft, but only very lightly coloured, then push the onion to one side of the pan.

Add the brains and break up into small pieces, and fry until lightly browned. Mix in with the onions.

Add the wine and plenty of seasonings and simmer gently for about 5 minutes, stirring from time to time.

Cut the slices of toast into halves or quarters and divide the brains among them. Sprinkle with paprika and garnish with parsley. Serve at once whilst hot.

SERVES 4

BRAISED SWEETBREADS

8 pairs sweetbreads
450 ml/¾ pint water
juice of 1 lemon
salt and black pepper

Sauce
25 g/1 oz butter or margarine
1 onion, peeled and chopped
2 carrots, peeled and chopped
1 bay leaf
2 tablespoons freshly chopped parsley
¼ teaspoon dried thyme
25 g/1 oz plain flour
600 ml/1 pint chicken stock
6 tablespoons medium sherry

Soak the sweetbreads in cold water for 20 minutes. Rinse and put into a saucepan with cold water to cover. Add the lemon juice and a good pinch of salt. Bring to the boil and simmer gently for 15 minutes.

Preheat the oven to fairly hot (200°C, 400°F, Gas Mark 6).

Drain and plunge the sweetbreads immediately into cold water to firm the meat. Remove the tubes and outer membrane and then flatten by standing a weighted plate on them.

For the sauce: melt the fat in a pan and add the onion, carrot, bay leaf and herbs and fry until the onion begins to brown. Add the flour, mix well and gradually add the stock, bringing up to the boil.

Place the sweetbreads in a casserole, pour the sauce over and season well. Cover tightly and cook in the preheated oven for 45 minutes, without a lid and basting occasionally.

Just before serving, stir in the sherry and adjust the seasonings. Serve with boiled rice and fresh vegetables.

SERVES 4

LIVER LOAF

1 onion, peeled and chopped
1 tablespoon oil
225 g/8 oz pigs' liver, cut into strips
50 g/2 oz streaky bacon, derinded
225 g/8 oz can tomatoes, drained
100 g/4 oz pork sausage meat
2 tablespoons tomato juice from the can
50 g/2 oz fresh breadcrumbs
1 teaspoon Worcestershire sauce
1 teaspoon dried mixed herbs or dried oregano
salt and black pepper
salads or vegetables, to garnish

Preheat the oven to fairly hot (200°C, 400°F, Gas Mark 6).

Fry the onion in the oil until soft. Add the liver and continue for 3–4 minutes until sealed and then add the bacon and continue for a further 2–3 minutes, stirring from time to time.

Mince or purée the liver, bacon and onion together with the tomatoes and turn into a bowl. Mix in the sausage meat, tomato juice, breadcrumbs, Worcestershire sauce, herbs and seasonings.

Turn into a greased 450 g/1 lb loaf tin and cover with greased foil.

Cook in the preheated oven for 45–60 minutes until the juices run clear when the loaf is pierced with a skewer.

Turn out the loaf and serve hot with boiled or fried potatoes and a green vegetable; or cool, chill and then turn out to serve cold in slices with salads.

SERVES 4

FARMHOUSE LIVER PÂTÉ

450 g/1 lb pigs' liver
300 g/10 oz streaky bacon rashers,
  derinded
1 large onion, peeled
2 garlic cloves, peeled and crushed
salt and black pepper
40 g/1½ oz fresh breadcrumbs
1 egg, beaten
2 tablespoons red wine, port or brandy
stuffed olives and watercress, to garnish

Preheat the oven to moderate (180°C, 350°F, Gas Mark 4).

Put the liver, half the bacon, and the onion and garlic through the fine blade of the mincer twice, or process in a food processor until very finely chopped.

Season very well and mix in the breadcrumbs and beaten egg, followed by the wine, port or brandy. Mix thoroughly.

Stretch the remaining bacon rashers with the back of a knife and use to line a greased 450 g/1 lb loaf tin.

Spoon in the liver mixture, level the top and fold the ends of the bacon over it.

Stand the loaf tin in a roasting tin containing about 2.5 cm/1 inch water and cook in the preheated oven for about 1¼ hours. Cool in the tin and then cover the top with double greaseproof paper and a heavy weight. Chill thoroughly.

Turn the pâté out carefully and garnish along the top with slices of stuffed olive and around the base with watercress. Serve with fingers of toast, crusty bread or crackers.

SERVES 6–8

LAMBS' TONGUES WITH SWEET SOUR SAUCE

4 lambs' tongues
900 ml/1½ pints beef stock
salt and black pepper

Sauce
1 tablespoon cornflour
150 ml/¼ pint cider
2 tablespoons brown sugar
1 tablespoon cranberry sauce
1 tablespoon soy sauce
2 tablespoons vinegar
parsley, to garnish

If using salted lambs' tongues, soak for 3–4 hours in cold water, or for fresh soak for 1–2 hours. Drain and place in a saucepan with the stock and seasonings and bring up to the boil. Cover and simmer for 1–1½ hours until very tender.

Drain the tongues, plunge into cold water and then skin. Cut each in half lengthwise.

Meanwhile, for the sauce: blend the cornflour with a little of the cider and pour into a saucepan. Add the rest of the cider, sugar, cranberry sauce and soy sauce and bring slowly to the boil.

Add a little of the tongue cooking liquor, season to taste and add the tongues. Reheat gently after adding the vinegar. Serve with freshly boiled rice or pasta, and garnished with parsley.

SERVES 4

DEVILLED TROTTERS

4 pigs' trotters
1 onion, peeled and quartered
1 bay leaf
strip of lemon rind
25 g/1 oz melted butter
cayenne pepper
dry mustard
garam masala

To garnish
fried or grilled mushrooms
watercress

Scrub the trotters and, if liked, split each in half lengthwise.

Place in a large saucepan with the onion and bay leaf and lemon rind. Cover with cold water and bring to the boil. Remove any scum from the surface, cover the pan and simmer for 2–2½ hours until tender.

Remove the trotters and drain well. The cooking liquor can be kept to use as stock for another dish.

Place the trotters in the grill pan with the skin side upwards. Brush all over with melted butter. Rub each with a little salt, cayenne pepper, dry mustard and garam masala until evenly coated.

Cook under a moderate grill until the trotters are golden brown and crisp. Serve with fried or grilled mushrooms, creamed potatoes and a garnish of watercress.

SERVES 4

INDEX

ACKNOWLEDGMENTS

SPECIAL PHOTOGRAPHY
Clive Streeter

FOOD PREPARED FOR PHOTOGRAPHY
Lyn Rutherford

STYLIST
Marian Price

ART DIRECTION
Bob Gordon

COLOUR ARTWORK
Nicky Kemball

BLACK AND WHITE ARTWORK
John Meadows

LINE AND PENCIL DRAWINGS
Sandra Pond

CONTRIBUTING AUTHOR
Rosemary Wadey

Some recipes and the photographs on pages 15, 22,
31, 39, 122, 123, 126, 130, 131, 135, 139, 143, 146, 151
and 155 supplied by British Meat.